S

D0865181

MARYLAND'S EASTERN SHORE

JOANNE MILLER

Contents

MARYLAND'S EASTERN SHORE

THE EASTERN SHORE

Maryland's Eastern Shore—also known as the upper Delmarva (DELaware, MARyland, and VirginiA) Peninsula—is bordered on the east by the Atlantic Ocean and Delaware Bay, and on the west by the mighty Chesapeake. If water views are what you're after, you'll achieve nirvana here. The peninsula has more than 7,000 miles of shoreline, hundreds of rivers, and thousands of acres of salt marshes—the Chesapeake is, after all, the largest inland estuary in the world. Several Wildlife Management areas touch the bay, including Blackwater, Fishing Bay, Ellis Bay, Deal Island, South Marsh Island north of Smith Island, and Cedar Island—all favored roosting places on the Atlantic flyway.

The bay is rich with opportunities for water recreation and is justly popular with boaters as well as landlubbers. From the Virginia border to the Bay Bridge, much of the southern central peninsula and northern part of Queen Anne's County that comprise Maryland's Eastern Shore continue to host small communities and vast farmland. A few cities—primarily Salisbury—have become more urbanized, though the population remains small.

Ocean City is a state unto itself. Once a spit of farmland, the area is now a playground for beach lovers, more like Miami than Maryland. However, there's plenty of fun to be found all over the Eastern Shore, whether you're seeking a quiet getaway or a social whirl.

HISTORY

For 11,000 years, the Eastern Shore was home to those who quietly farmed, hunted, and

HIGHLIGHTS

◖ **Chesapeake Bay Maritime Museum:** Anyone interested in maritime history must visit this museum in St. Michaels which features more than 20 buildings of interactive exhibits on more than 18 acres; you'll find information on boat building, historic boats, decoys, and Chesapeake Bay life. Several historic vessels, such as the skipjack *Rosie Parks* and the log-bottom Bugeye *Edna E. Lockwood*, are docked on the waterfront (page 19).

◖ **Islands and Towns Tour:** This driving tour is a feast for the eyes. Travelers journey on a scenic route around the best of the area, starting in the attractive town of Cambridge and winding on back roads through Blackwater National Refuge, the watermen's community of Hooper's Island, and a variety of villages and buildings raised during European settlement — including Old Trinity Church on Taylor's Island, built between 1675 and 1690 (page 33).

◖ **Ward Museum of Wildfowl Art:** Visitors have to remind themselves that they are looking at carved and painted wood, not wild birds in flight. The work is extraordinary, as you might expect from the premier collection of wildfowl art in the world. The museum examines the history and heritage of the art, from antique working decoys to contemporary carvings (page 37).

◖ **Gov. J. Millard Tawes Historical Museum:** Set in the ultimate waterman's town and built on decades of oyster shells, the Governor J. Millard Tawes Historical Museum offers an intimate portrait of life in a port town. Guided walking tours are available from the Port of Crisfield (page 42).

◖ **Ocean City Boardwalk:** Stretching from the inlet north past 27th Street, the boardwalk functions as a chronological history of this fishing village/resort. The oldest and most active part of the boardwalk is between the inlet on South 1st Street and 8th Street, which includes the informative Ocean City Life-Saving Station Museum. People-watching, shops, all sorts of food concessions and rides and games make up a great place to spend a day or week (page 53).

LOOK FOR ◖ TO FIND RECOMMENDED SIGHTS, ACTIVITIES, DINING, AND LODGING.

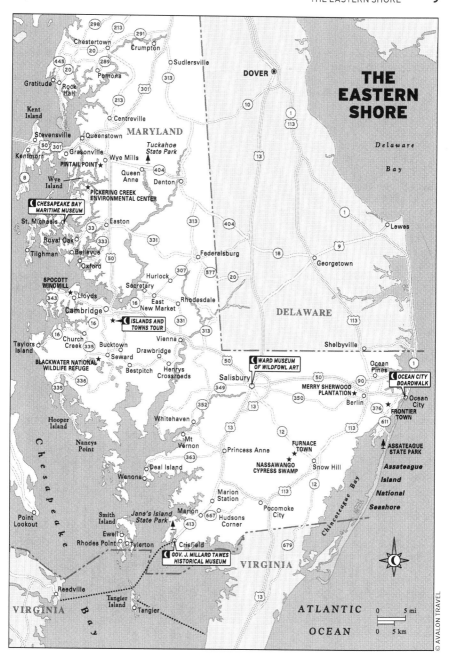

© AVALON TRAVEL

exploited the rich resources of the Chesapeake. Captain John Smith met the peaceful Algonquin-speaking Ozinies in what was to become Queen Anne's County in 1608 or 1609. Some 25 years later, William Claiborne established a trading fort on Kent Island—the first settlement in the state. Claiborne claimed that the territory belonged to Virginia; Lord Calvert insisted it was his, and the Ozinies and other natives left the area to escape the din of battle. Calvert won out, and British settlers followed the rivers and shorelines to clear the land for tobacco planting. In the early 1600s, one pound of the leaf could fetch more than double an average English sharecropper's annual income. Tobacco as a cash crop was so prevalent by the 18th century that it was used as money, and prices for most commodities were quoted in pounds of tobacco. Plantations grew along the rivers, and the rivers were the highways of the time.

Queen Anne's County was formally established in 1708, with the county seat at Queen Anne's Town (Queenstown). Within a few years, it was moved up the Corsica River to Centreville, which has the oldest courthouse in continuous use in Maryland (built in 1792).

By 1760, transatlantic tobacco trade prices were fluctuating wildly; many planters shifted to the blue-chip agricultural product of grain. The haphazard tobacco fields gave way to today's broad, orderly fields, and linked the Eastern Shore to northern markets, chiefly Philadelphia. Merchants from that area invested in local mills, including the Wye Mill, in order to control production and prices. Market towns like Centreville grew to reflect the bustling trade activity, and by 1820, 80 percent of arable land was under cultivation.

The industrial revolution brought steam power, and farm machinery increased productivity. At the same time, steam replaced sail and opened regional markets on the Chesapeake and Delaware Bays for produce, oysters, and fish. Steamboats plied the rivers of the Eastern Shore, and linked small towns with the outside world. Railroad lines were built throughout the region in the 1870s, and fishing and oyster-ing boomed. Kent Narrows and Kent Island became important seafood processing centers, with as many as 12 packing houses operating at one time.

By the 1920s, steamboats themselves were obsolete, replaced by railroads. And the iron horse gave way to iron horsepower—automobiles—by the 1950s. Lifestyles remained slow on the Eastern Shore until 1952, when the completion of the first Chesapeake Bay Bridge ushered in rapid business, industrial, and real estate development.

ORIENTATION

Maryland's Eastern Shore covers a lot of (marshy) ground. Chesapeake Bay inundates the land, dividing it into hundreds of small bays and inlets. Rivers thread the entire peninsula, giving it the best of fresh- and salt-water environments. The main route, U.S. 50, crosses the Bay Bridge, slides down the coast to Cambridge, then hikes straight away east to Ocean City. U.S. 13 hops out of Delaware near Salisbury and runs south all the way to Crisfield.

The western side of the peninsula holds many smaller towns, all of which are attractive to boaters and landsmen for their antiques, rural surroundings, and outdoor recreation opportunities. In the southern part of the peninsula, Crisfield is an angler's paradise. The "interior"—including the villages of White Haven, Pocomoke, Snow Hill, and Berlin—is separated by wide swaths of farmland, streams and rivers. Salisbury, the "big city" of the Eastern Shore is a good place to base if you choose to spend your time in between the more populous areas, and want to explore the roads less traveled.

On the farthest reaches of Maryland's Eastern Shore, Ocean City becomes *the* big city only in the summer. It's made for family vacations and every rendition of beach life, from luxurious to casual beach bum.

PLANNING YOUR TIME

Whether you're coming up U.S. 13 from Virginia or traveling south on U.S. 50 from the Bay Bridge, the Eastern Shore of Maryland is a place to be savored slowly. You'll need a week to 10 days to appreciate the counties that make up the quintessential Tidewater—longer if you intend to take advantage of the fine cycling routes, particularly in Dorchester, Talbot, and Queen Anne's Counties. All of these areas are accessible by boat. Ocean City is the biggest and best-known destination on the Eastern Shore. It requires a week of your time just to work on your tan and your kite-flying skills.

As a first or last stop in contrast to the faster pace of Baltimore, plan a day in Queen Anne's County at **Wye and Environs,** including **Wye Mill,** a hike on **Wye Island,** and a snack pack from **Orrell's Maryland Beaten Biscuits** for a fillip of Eastern Shore ease. Stay in nearby **Queen Anne.** You can take the beautiful Tidewater farms, gentle pace of life, and quiet countryside home with you, at least in memory.

Though it's a tourist town, **St. Michaels,** in Talbot County, features the **Chesapeake Bay Maritime Museum,** a couple of hours of interest to anyone who loves the bay and boats. Make sure to visit the other towns in the area, particularly charming **Oxford** and **Easton** (stay for dinner). Two to three days in the area should give you plenty of time to see this well-loved part of the bay, and lodging and restaurant opportunities are plentiful.

Head south to Dorchester County, using **Cambridge** as a base for the **Islands and Towns Tour** (three hours of travel time) that includes **Blackwater National Wildlife Refuge.** This is also a good opportunity to enjoy the restaurant, spa, and golf course at the **Hyatt Regency.** Plan on at least two days here.

Schedule another two to three days in **Salisbury,** Wicomico County, for the **Ward Museum of Wildfowl Art** (two–three hours), the **Salisbury Zoo** (one hour), and the **Whitehaven Loop** (two hours of travel time), with dinner at the **Red Roost** and possibly an overnight in quiet **Whitehaven.**

In Somerset County, a stop in **Crisfield** should take two to three days—for the **Port of Crisfield Escorted Walking Tour** at the **Gov. J. Millard Tawes Historical Museum** (two hours) and a little fishing and shopping, while enjoying the beaches and trails of **Jane's**

Island State Park. Camping is particularly attractive here.

Worchester County's biggest attraction is **Ocean City,** a major destination. A week or more should be planned for laying around on the beach, playing miniature golf, eating seafood ad infinitum, and exploring the surrounding area. Day trips could include a trip down to Snow Hill and **Furnace Town** for a little history (two hours) and a canoe trip through peaceful marshlands (day-long). **Assateague Island** is an all-day must-see, if only for the adorable ponies.

FESTIVALS AND EVENTS

Ocean City holds events year-round in its convention center, including a big boat show in February. Many events are handled by individuals, so the listed phone numbers may not be accurate—call the local convention and visitors bureau at 800/OC-OCEAN (800/626-2326) for an updated list. St. Michaels Business Association (800/808-7622, www.stmichaelsmd.org) sponsors events around all major holidays, especially Halloween and Christmas.

In late March or early April, the prestigious **Ward World Championship Wildfowl Carving Competition** (Salisbury, 410/742-4988), held since 1970, includes a weekend of activities.

Get those arms in shape for the **Nanticoke River Canoe and Kayak Race,** an 8.1-mile course from Mardela Springs to Vienna at the end of April. This is the first in five races that make up the Delmarva Circuit.

The first week in May, **Spring Fest** (800/626-2326) is the "official" opening weekend of Ocean City. Four days of activities include entertainment, arts, crafts and food. The end of September or beginning of October is the official "closing" of the beach, and **Sunfest** is the four-day party that ends the summer with a bang.

The **Annual Antique & Classic Boat Festival** (410/745-2916), held at the Chesapeake Bay Maritime Museum in St. Michaels, features more than 100 classic boats and automobiles in a judged show. There are also seminars and special exhibits, free with admission.

In July, the **Tuckahoe Steam and Gas Show** (410/822-9868) in Easton features the huffing and puffing of a variety of antique steam engines, gas engines, blacksmith displays, a museum, a horse pull, and an auction.

The annual **Thunder on the Narrows** (http://kentnarrowsracing.com), in Kent Narrows, features hydroplane and speed skiff racing in August.

Also in August, Ocean City's **White Marlin Open** (800/626-2326, www.whitemarlinopen .com) offers cash prizes of $850,000, with more than 250 boats competing for record-setting catches of white marlin, blue marlin, wahoo, tuna, and shark.

The Annual Skipjack Races & Festival (410/784-2811 or 800/521-9189, www.skipjack .net/races) is held Labor Day weekend in September on Deal Island. Food, arts and crafts, and family activities are offered.

The **Pemberton Colonial Fair** (410/742-1741), held outside Salisbury, combines 18th-century games, performances (including period dancing, and dressage and other horse events), and booths in an authentic country manor house and grounds.

Olde Princess Anne Days (800/521-9189, www.visitsomerset.com/events) have been held since the late 1950s and remain as popular as ever. The historic house and garden tour and colonial fair takes place over two days in October.

Furnace Town, near Snow Hill, hosts the **Chesapeake Celtic Festival** (410/632-2032) in October. It features music, dancing, sheep-herding, a medieval encampment, and food and crafts vendors.

In November, the **Waterfowl Festival** (www .waterfowlfestival.org) takes over the town of Easton (the streets are closed and decorated). This is one of the biggest events on the Eastern Shore, featuring art, sculpture, duck stamps, crafts, demonstrations, food, music, and more.

Ocean City sponsors a big **Christmas Parade** (410/524-9000) each year, featuring floats, bands, motorcycles, and all relevant Clauses.

GETTING THERE AND AROUND
By Air

Commuter airlines service the Salisbury airport from Baltimore and Washington, D.C., but that remains the only air access other than small planes. There is a small airport in Ocean City, and **regional airports** on Kent Island and in Easton and Cambridge, as well as in the vicinity of Salisbury and Crisfield. Commuter flights are available from BWI in Baltimore and all major airports in the Washington, D.C., area.

By Bus

Greyhound Bus (800/229-9424, www.grey hound.com) service is available to Stevensville (Kent Island), Easton, St. Michaels, Cambridge, Salisbury, Crisfield, Princess Anne, and Ocean City, with limited service to Vienna.

For local intra-city transportation, **Shore Transit** (443/260-2300, www.shoretransit .org) offers limited regional routes in Somerset, Wicomico, Dorchester, and Worcester Counties on Maryland's lower Eastern Shore. Caroline, Dorchester, Kent, Talbot and Queen Anne's Counties are served by **Maryland Upper Shore Transit** (MUST, 866/330-6878, www.mustbus.info).Generally, the exact fare of $1–2 is required.

By Car

Main car access to the Delmarva Peninsula from the west is the Bay Bridge, U.S. 50, which reaches all the way to Ocean City. The area is very spread out—for sightseeing, a car is really the only option. U.S. 13, which begins in Delaware, is the main north–south route. Other roads are generally well-maintained two-lane blacktop.

Wye Island and Vicinity

The area around the Wye River came to the attention of many Americans in the 1990s as the site of a series of peace talks between Israeli and Palestinian leaders hosted by President Clinton. The talks took place in a private plantation home on Wye Island.

SIGHTS
Wye Island NRMA

The entire island is designated a Natural Resource Management Area. Located at the end of Carmichael Road, Wye Island consists of a number of private homes in a scenic jewel of a rustic setting. There are turnoffs on the single road where visitors may park their cars and walk tree-lined lanes filled with songbirds, including the rare indigo bunting. The state of Maryland purchased the 2,450-acre island in the 1970s, when the original 13 farms were in danger of being broken up for development.

Village of Wye

The village, on Route 662, is home to the **Wye Grist Mill** (14296 Old Wye Mills Rd./Rte. 662, 410/827-3850, 10 A.M.–4 P.M. Thurs.–Sun. mid-Apr.–early Nov., $2), one of the earliest and most authentic industrial sites in Maryland. On the first and third Saturday of the month, volunteers demonstrate the traditional stone grinding process.

A mill has been operating on the site for more than 300 years. In fact, the milling operations were significant enough that the Maryland General Assembly of 1706 created Queen Anne's County using the mill as a reference point. In 1956, the mill and one acre were deeded by the state to Preservation Maryland. Today, the mill grinds Eastern Shore corn and wheat and Pennsylvania buckwheat by the traditional stone method using water power only, and visitors may purchase the flours. The small mill is a perfectly preserved example of colonial era technology, right down to the conduit pipes made of boards battened together. A video and exhibit chronicle the Eastern Shore's role in the

A LONG WAY FROM HAVANA

In April 2000, Wye Island became another sort of refuge. Elian Gonzalez, along with his father, stepmother, and baby half-brother, moved to a two-story white farmhouse on the grounds of the secluded Wye River Conference Center, the 1,100-acre estate that was home to one of the state's first governors, William Paca. The conference center, 70 miles east of Washington, is perhaps best known as the site of the Middle East peace negotiations in 1996 and 1998. The Gonzalez family was awaiting court action on whether the six-year-old boy should be granted an asylum hearing or be allowed to return with his father to his birthplace.

Elian was a survivor of a shipload of Cuban refugees that sank off the coast of Florida, and became a cause célèbre when relatives in the Miami Cuban community insisted that he stay in the United States rather than return home to his father and Castro's Cuba.

Before being moved to Wye Island, Elian's Cuban family had been staying at Andrews Air Force Base since their arrival in the United States. To reunite the family, Elian was forcibly removed from the home of his Miami relatives.

One neighbor said he didn't think Elian's visit caused nearly the commotion of the 1998 peace talks, when Secret Service agents shut down the road leading to the estate. "That's the only time we had security that high, when the president was here," said Kevin Compton, operations manager at Pintail Point Farm. "There's constantly stuff going on down there that requires security, but we don't ever feel it."

Elian returned to Cuba with his father at the end of June 2000.

19th-century agricultural boom. Each year, on the Saturday nearest June 26, Wye Mill hosts a harvest craft fair.

The 96-foot tall **Wye Oak,** south of the grist mill in the village, was a sight to behold. The tree had been around since 1540—it pushed up out of the ground barely 50 years after Columbus reputedly set foot on American soil. When Europeans first explored the upper regions of the Chesapeake Bay, this white oak was already fully mature. In 1909, the tree was recorded as the largest white oak specimen in the eastern United States—it was 32 feet in circumference, with a crown spread of 119 feet. Windfall was a continual threat to the old timer; over 100 cables intertwined throughout the crown to prevent the stiff limbs from snapping during high winds. In 2002, the Wye Oak lost its final battle with the elements and came down. Seedlings were planted at Mount Vernon and in 29-acre Wye Oak State Park behind the tree prior to its fall. Near the site of the old tree, a small brick building, **Wye School,** may have also been used as a plantation office or dwelling. Just down the road is the still-active **Old Wye Church,** built in 1717 and restored in the 1940s.

RECREATION
Pintail Point at
The River Plantation
On the way to Wye Island (511 Pintail Point Ln., Queenstown, 410/827-7029, www.pintail point.com), Pintail Point is a sort of Disneyland for sportsmen. The property has the look of a very wealthy private retreat and offers deluxe lodging (see the *Accommodations* section in this chapter) and extensive fishing, hunting, and sporting clay activities. Guests may take any of a number of fly-fishing classes, from casting to fly-tying, and may fish in the freshwater ponds on the property or take one of several charters out on the Chesapeake. Hunters can pursue deer, wild duck, sea duck, and dove hunting in season, or take advantage of Pintail's hunting preserve. Guests may bring their own dogs, or select one from the facility's kennels. Those more interested in sport shooting—golf with a gun—enjoy Pintail's

22-station shooting clay range. The "Cast and Blast" package features a half day of charter boat fishing, lunch, and a round of 50 targets on the sporting clay course. All equipment may be rented. The River Plantation also manages Hunters Oak Golf Club (500 Amberly Lane, Queenstown, 800/697-1777), for those who prefer the traditional game.

ACCOMMODATIONS AND FOOD
◀ **Pintail Point** (511 Pintail Point Ln., Queenstown, 410/827-7065, $185–500) offers guests several sporting activities and beautiful accommodations. Because of the isolated rural setting, visitors who have no interest in sports can still enjoy a quiet retreat. There are two bed-and-breakfast locations on the property. A 1936 English Tudor, the Manor House, is surrounded by gardens and walking paths along the Wye River. Three rooms, one suite, and a cottage, all with private baths, are available. Irishtown, an early-1900s farmhouse with three bedrooms and two baths, rents at $500 per night for the entire house.

A visit to Wye wouldn't be complete without a stop at **Orrell's Maryland Beaten Biscuits** (Rte. 662 next to the Old Wye Church, 410/822-2065, www.beatenbiscuits .bizland.com). Hot biscuits are available at the shop 9 A.M.–1 P.M. every Tuesday and Wednesday, and Orrell's might be open at other times—call if you're in the area. If you've never had a beaten biscuit, the first bite might be a shock: Even fresh out of the oven, the exterior is more reminiscent of granite than flour and water. The inside, however, is as tender and light as goose down. "Beaten," to me, means pummeled with a spoon—these biscuits date back to the plantation era, when leavening was in short supply and the term "beaten" was literal. Some cooks used a hammer, some the back of an axe—at Orrell's, the preferred instrument is a baseball bat. One old recipe states, "Beat 30 minutes for family and 45 for company." As you might expect, everyone at Orrell's is very mellow. Ruth Orrell began the biscuit business in 1935 using her mother's recipe, and the little bakery employs many of the neighboring women, who sit around the table in flowered aprons chatting and pinching off dough into biscuit-sized balls. Nothing settles an upset stomach faster, and odd as they may seem at first bite ("Should I eat it or skip it across the lake?"), they definitely grow on you. Ruth has a hefty business shipping biscuits all over the country. Call her or log onto her website and she'll send you a dozen or more of regular, honey, cheese, cayenne and cheese, or flat.

Greater Queen Anne's County

This county, which includes the Bay Bridge, Kent Island, and the gateway to the Eastern Shore, remains largely farmland, with a few small towns and commercial centers.

SIGHTS
Horsehead Wetlands Center
The center, administered by the Wildfowl Trust of North America (Perry Corner Rd., Grasonville, 410/827-6694, 9 A.M.–5 P.M. daily except major holidays, $5 adults, $4 seniors, $2 kids 18 and under) is composed of six distinct wetland habitats in 500 acres.

The Wildfowl Trust was established in 1979 by a group of conservationists who modeled it after similar organizations in the United Kingdom. The Grasonville property's original purpose was waterfowl research, though it's now used to study migratory behavior and patterns, and serves as an education and information center. Migrating birds pass through the property seasonally, and a captive population of waterfowl and raptors is kept on the property—many are birds that were injured in the wild and were unable to survive on their own, such as a blind owl and an eagle with an injured wing. The center offers an environmental science camp and other educational programs throughout the year. Four easy trails, all less than a mile, lead visitors through differing habitats and gardens. Several ponds and lakes are home to turtles and other amphibians, and the surrounding marshes support wildflowers and butterflies. A visitors center offers information on the wide variety of birds that pass through the area, and also has a small, well-stocked gift shop.

Queen Anne's
Museum of Eastern Shore Life
This small museum (126 Dulin Clark Rd., Centreville, 410/758-8641) displays artifacts, household furnishings, and farmers' and watermen's gear from the past and present. Exhibits focus on rural life on the Eastern Shore. This is one of several historic sites administered by the Historic Sites Consortium of Queen Anne's County (888/400-7787). Others include the Tucker House, Wright's Chance, and the county courthouse in Centreville; the Cray House, old post office, and train depot in Stevensville; the colonial courthouse in Queenstown; Dudley's Chapel and the train station in Sudlersville; the Wye grist mill; and the Church Hill theater. If local history interests you, order an excellent free brochure, "Explore Our History and Heritage," by contacting the Historic Sites consortium (410/604-2100 or 888/400-7787, hsc@historicqac.org) with your name and address. You can also get one from the Office of Tourism (425 Piney Narrows Rd., 410/604-2100, www.qac.org/depts/tourism).

SHOPPING
Chesapeake Outlet Village (Rte. 301, Queenstown) will satisfy your needs for a quick outlet-shopping fix on the Eastern Shore. All the standards are there: Mikasa, Jones New York, Dansk, and more. Most shops are open daily.

Chesapeake Antique Center (www.chesapeakeantiques.com, open daily), adjacent to the Chesapeake Outlet Village on Route 301, is a multi-dealer antiques marketplace with a little of everything.

Though it's on the border of Queen Anne's

and Kent Counties, **Dixon's Furniture Auction** (intersection of Rte. 544 and Rte. 290, Crumpton, 410/928-3006) is worth a special trip. A public auction takes place every Wednesday. It offers a mountain of goods of every quality and description in three "areas"— good, better, and best, with base prices gauged accordingly, from $15 up. A live auctioneer goes over the merchandise piece by piece and tends to move fast, but be prepared to wait if the merchandise you want sits on the tables farthest from the front.

Kent Fort Farm (135 Eastern Ln., Stevensville, 410/643-1650, 9 A.M.–5 P.M. Wed. and Fri.–Sat., 10 A.M.–4 P.M. Sun. early summer–fall, weekends only in Oct.) is a great place to take the kids. It offers a variety of pick-your-own fruit. There's an annual peach festival the first Saturday in August, and a pumpkin patch on October weekends. Please note: This is a cash-only business.

RECREATION
Tuckahoe State Park
Tuckahoe Creek runs through the length of this park (13070 Crouse Mill Rd., Queen Anne, 410/820-1668). A lake offers boating and fishing, and the Adkins Arboretum encompasses 500 acres of park land and almost three miles of surfaced walkways leading through the tagged native species of trees and shrubs. The park offers scenic hiking, biking and equestrian trails, flat water canoeing, Visitors take advantage of numerous seasonal activities, such as bird watching and guided walks. Pets are allowed in the family camping area and most of the park, except the lake area, as long as they remain on a leash.

Boating and Canoeing: Canoeing at Tuckahoe is a popular activity on both the 60-acre lake and the creek because of the park's abundant wildlife. Visitors share space with bald eagles, ospreys, and great blue herons; beavers and muskrats have surprised visitors by swimming past their canoes. Tuckahoe is full of pockets of secluded beauty, some accessible only by canoe. Canoes, kayaks, and paddle boats may be rented for a daily fee. Guided canoe trips on both the lake and the Tuckahoe Creek are offered throughout the year by the park naturalist. Gasoline motor use is prohibited.

Hiking, Biking, and Horses: Tuckahoe boasts 20 miles of excellent hiking, biking, and equestrian trails, such as the Tuckahoe Valley Trail, a self-guided Natural Trail, the Physical Fitness Trail, and the Lake Trail.

Camping: The park offers 51 single-family sites, 33 with electric hookups, and a central bathhouse. In addition, there's a youth group camping area with four sites, each site accommodating up to 30 people with a central bathhouse with showers and toilet facilities. Four camper (rustic) cabins are available; each cabin sleeps four and is equipped with a ceiling fan, electricity, and air conditioning, but no running water. Call 888/432-2267 for reservations.

Getting There: Tuckahoe State Park is located approximately 35 miles east of the Bay Bridge, just off Route 404. Travel east on Route 50/301 across the Bay Bridge. Route 50/301 splits; bear to the right on Route 50. Make a left at the intersection of Routes 50 and 404. Go approximately eight miles to the intersection of Routes 404 and 480. Make a left on Route 480. Eveland Road is on your immediate left. Once on Eveland Road, follow the directional signs.

ACCOMMODATIONS
◖**Kent Manor Inn** (500 Kent Manor Dr., Rte. 8 south, Stevensville, Kent Island, 410/643-5757 or 800/820-4511, www.kentmanor.com, $180–265) was established on one of the oldest tracts of land in Maryland, dating back to 1651. The main section of the current hotel was built in 1820. More than 226 acres of the original farm surround the manor house, and all rooms in the gracious (and completely modernized) inn have a water view, private bath, and telephone. Kent Manor Inn has been designated a "Historic Hotel of America" by the National Trust for Historic Preservation. The elegant building, with its expansive lawns and gardens, is frequently a site for weddings. The inn also offers formal lunch and dinner in their first floor dining room; in summer, the win-

dows look out on the lawns and inlet, and in winter, the Victorian fireplaces fill the space with warmth and light. The dining room is open to the public.

Stillwater Inn Bed & Breakfast (7109 2nd Ave., Queenstown, 410/827-9362, $125) is a stroll away from Queenstown Creek. This charming, airy, country-style B&B was built in 1904 for a local doctor, and sometimes served as the vestry of Wye parish before becoming a bed-and-breakfast. Both of the guestrooms have a private bath. The innkeepers, Kevin and Linda Vasbinder, serve a full country breakfast in the morning (included in room rate); Kevin's library may contain every fantasy book ever written, and it's tempting to sink into a world of sword and sorcery. Guests will enjoy the lovely private garden in the warmer months. It's a good idea to get directions from the innkeepers, as many of the streets of Queenstown were modified from narrow alleys and don't necessarily connect in a logical way. The old town area seems a million miles away from busy Route 301, though it's less than one mile.

FOOD
Quick and Cheap

Though the Kent Narrows and surrounding area are famous for big seafood restaurants, there are a few inexpensive places to eat that are quite good. Anyone who's crossed the bridge more than once knows ❬ **Holly's** (five miles east of the bridge on Rte. 50 in Grasonville, 410/827-8711, 7 A.M.–9:30 P.M. daily, $7–18). This Eastern Shore institution is a restaurant and motel, opened by the Ewing family in 1955. Judging from the decor and the prices, Holly's remains firmly in the '50s; you'll barely have time to name more than a few states and their capitals (the placemats quiz your geographical knowledge) before your fried chicken special arrives. Even if your U.S. geography is rusty (where exactly is Missouri?), the food will make you feel smart. Real milkshakes and whole apple dumplings star on the diner-style menu, and most salads and sandwiches run under $7.

Chesapeake Chicken & Rockin' Ribs (on the north side of Rte. 50 at 101 Hissey Rd., seven miles east of the bridge, 410/827-0030, lunch and dinner daily) is a locally owned barbecue joint with tasty platters. Chicken with two sides is under $11, ribs and two sides are $15. You can eat in the cheerful dining room or get everything to go—party platters that serve up to 40 people are a specialty. It also offers excellent chicken soup and salads.

Bob's Mini Mart & Deli (102 Clay Dr., Queenstown, 410/827-8780, 5:30 A.M.–8 P.M. Mon.–Sat., $5 and under) isn't fancy, but the sandwiches, subs, and salads are good, and everything is prepared to order. The prices rival fast food. Yes, it's in a gas station, but there's a separate sit-down dining area. This is the place where the locals eat, and it's often very crowded around lunchtime.

Seafood

The large seafood eateries on Kent Island on the east end of the bridge range in quality and price. **Annie's** (500 Kent Narrows Way, 410/827-7103, lunch and dinner daily, salads and sandwiches $8, dinner $22) doesn't specialize—the menu is several pages long and includes all the local seafood dishes (steamed clams, crab cakes), Angus beef, sandwiches, salads, and Italian specialties (a local favorite). This is a big, casual place, with big plates—not gourmet, but perfect for the hearty eater who wants a lot of choices. Reservations are accepted.

❬ **The Narrows** (3023 Kent Narrows Way S., Grasonville, 410/827-8113, www.thenarrows restaurant.com, lunch and dinner daily, $10–27) has an elegant feel without being stuffy, and the menu is sophisticated and well prepared. Lunch features items such as a steak-and-brie sandwich and pecan-crusted catfish, and dinner offers grilled chicken Oscar and filet mignon with broiled crab cakes, among other dishes. It also serves light suppers—a petite version of regular menu items for a few dollars less. Reservations are recommended.

Drive a few miles down Kent Island on Route 8, and you'll come to Kentmorr Road, which leads to a planned development built around a private airport. Many of the homes

crabs packed for shipping

have airplanes parked nearby, and at the end of the road, you'll find **Kentmorr** (910 Kentmorr Rd., Stevensville, 410/643-2263, www.kent morr.com, 11:30 A.M.–9 P.M. daily, $7–25), an upscale neighborhood restaurant with spectacular views and a broad menu. Though the place is out of the way, it's very popular. The menu features steamed crabs, a raw bar, prepared seafood dishes, chicken and beef, and soups, pasta, and salads. The chef will barbecue your choice of meat, and prime rib is

a specialty. The Sunday breakfast buffet is a local favorite. Dinner choices include chicken, steak with crab cake, and steamed crabs (market price).

INFORMATION

Questions about Queen Anne's can be answered by the **Queen Anne's County Office of Tourism** (425 Piney Narrows Rd., Chester, MD 21619, 410/604-2100, www.qac.org/depts/ tourism). You can order a visitors guide online.

St. Michaels

Founded in 1677, this county was once a haven for shipbuilders, privateers, and blockade-runners. St. Michaels prides itself on civic cooperation during the War of 1812. When British marines converged for a night attack on the town's shipyards in 1813, the forewarned residents doused their lights and hung lanterns in trees and masts, drawing fire away from the

town—only one house was hit. Shortly after, Frederick Douglass—born near Tuckahoe Creek—lived as a slave in St. Michaels in 1830. He taught at a clandestine school for blacks here, then escaped to freedom in 1836.

These days, the town is a destination for pleasure boaters and yachts flying international colors. *Power & Motoryacht Magazine* named St.

Michaels as one of America's favorite anchorages, out of 12 including Desolation Sound in British Columbia and Bimini in the Bahamas. During the summer, the town is bustling, though the action slows down markedly by October.

SIGHTS
◖ Chesapeake Bay Maritime Museum

This sprawling enterprise (end of Mill St., Navy Point, 410/745-2916, www.cbmm.org, 10 A.M.–5 P.M. daily spring and autumn, until 6 P.M. in summer, until 4 P.M. in winter, $10 adults, $9 seniors, $5 children ages 6–17) is one of Maryland's top cultural attractions, and a major attraction on the Eastern Shore.

Twenty-three buildings contain interactive exhibits on boat building, historic boats, decoys, and Chesapeake Bay life. The museum spreads over 18 acres, and several historic vessels, such as the skipjack *Rosie Parks* and the log-bottom bugeye *Edna E. Lockwood,* are docked on the waterfront. The Hooper Strait Lighthouse, a fully restored 1879 screwpile wooden structure, is one of the most popular exhibits. Visitors can climb the narrow stairs, visit the living quarters, and see the Fresnel lens that surrounds the light on the top deck—it's the second largest size ever made. The octagonal lighthouse was moved from its former location several miles out in Chesapeake Bay when it was scheduled for destruction in the mid-1960s. The museum offers families overnight stays in the lighthouse during the summer.

On Tuesdays and Thursdays, the workshops are busy with the sounds of volunteers (more than 300 of them) repairing and maintaining the museum's all-wood boat collection. Much of the wood—mostly white cedar—is donated.

The museum sponsors a number of special events throughout the year. Of note are the Arts Festival, Antique and Classic Boat Festival (see *Festivals and Events* in this chapter), and an Antique and Classic Boat Festival in June, the largest of its kind. This event displays boats (from 80-foot yachts to 15-foot working skiffs), models, books, and boat races. The museum shop is well stocked with toys, souvenirs, and books about boats and Chesapeake Bay life.

© JOANNE MILLER

skipjack at Chesapeake Bay Maritime Museum

LOG CANOES AND SKIPJACKS

Water transport on the Chesapeake was developed to meet a number of needs, from swift transportation to food gathering. Most of the bay and the many rivers that feed it are quite shallow (less than 10 feet). Wind-powered watercraft with shallow drafts were a necessity, and working boats also needed to be speed-controlled. The typical Chesapeake working vessel is wide, shallow, and heavy.

Log canoes were modified from the common form of Native American transportation, burned and hollowed-out logs. Builders lashed together several of these logs to form a hull, then placed decking over the logs and built up planks from the sides. Three- and five-log canoes were common. An unusual nine-log canoe is restored at the Maritime Museum in St. Michaels, which also sponsors log canoe races throughout the summer. Log canoes built for working watermen were sometimes referred to as bugeyes, thought to be a corruption of "buckie" or "pungie," the Scottish word for oyster in colonial times.

Skipjacks are broad, shallow-draft sailing vessels made especially for oystering. Their slow and steady pace permitted watermen to drag a 12- to 15-foot-long set of "tongs" behind the boat and pull the mollusks off the bottom.

SHOPPING

Talbot Street, the main street in town, is lined with antiques and collectible shops, clothing stores, bookstores, and every imaginable outlet for spending money. Many of the shops are open only during the high season, roughly mid-April to November. Of note are the **Mind's Eye** (205 S. Talbot, 410/745-2023), a contemporary crafts gallery, and **Chesapeake Trading Co.** (102 S. Talbot St., 410/745-9797) a good place to find all things Chesapeake.

RECREATION

Landlubbers can get two-wheeled transportation courtesy of **St. Michaels Town Dock Marina** (305 Mulberry St., 410/745-2400). The marina rents single bicycles.

Tours

The glass-enclosed 65-foot *Patriot* cruises the Miles River, and during the one-hour outing, covers Talbot County history and Chesapeake lore (410/745-3100, www.patriotcruises.com). There's a snack and booze bar on board. You can catch the boat at 11 A.M., 12:30 P.M., 2:30 P.M., and 4 P.M. daily April–November. Captain Dave points out clammers, crabbers, and stately homes. It's docked next to the Maritime Museum, and ticket prices are $10 for adults, $4.50 for kids under 12.

Ed Farley welcomes visitors aboard his skipjack *H. M. Krentz* (410/745-6080, www.oystercatcher.com) for a two-hour sail mid-April–October ($30). Captain Farley, a working waterman, gives a lively commentary about life in and around the Chesapeake.

Dockside Express Land & Sea Tours of St. Michaels (P.O. Box 122, Tilghman, 888/312-7847, www.docksideexpress.com, $10 per person, by advance reservation only) features costumed guides who escort visitors for a one-hour walk around St. Michaels. The tour focuses on local history.

And, if a steady equestrian pace is appealing, try a horse-drawn carriage ride from **Chesapeake Carriage Company** (9072 New Rd., 410/745-4011); reservations are required.

ACCOMMODATIONS

St. Michaels has dozens of inns and B&Bs, as you might expect from a summer tourist mecca. Lodgings on the main street, Talbot, cost less but experience fairly constant traffic until the wee hours during the summer.

$100-150

The Parsonage Inn (210 N. Talbot St., 410/745-5519 or 800/394-5519, www.parsonage-inn.com, $100–195) suffers slightly from a location problem, but makes up for it with lovely brick Victorian architecture and pretty rooms.

The former owner, Dr. Henry Dodson, established the local brickyard in 1877 and built the house to show off different patterns in 1883. All eight rooms have private baths and include breakfast. Three rooms feature fireplaces.

The **George Brooks House** (24500 Rolles Range Rd., 410/745-0999, www.georgebrooks house.com, $95–225) earned the Historical Society of Talbot County's Heritage Award for best historic renovation. This 1908 Gothic Revival Victorian is named for its builder, an African American entrepreneur and author on race relations whose successful business ventures provided this home and care for his 11 orphaned nieces and nephews. Each of six bedrooms features a private bath, hand-carved mahogany furniture, and Waverly fabrics on the bed and windows. The seven-acre property also has formal gardens and an outdoor pool. Rooms include a gourmet breakfast.

$150-250

Two historic properties were restored and joined to create **Five Gables Inn & Spa** (202 N. Talbot

LEGAL PIRACY

Too small and poor to equip a proper navy that could seriously threaten the Royal Navy during the War of 1812, the U.S. government relied on Yankee ingenuity. Congress encouraged ship owners, especially those of American merchant vessels designed to be fast on American waterways, to enlist their assets in the fight. American merchant vessels built in the colonies were designed to be fast and maneuverable on American waterways. Ships built in Fell's Point, Baltimore, were especially suitable – topsail schooners later dubbed Baltimore clippers. The experienced seamen who sailed them were not at all interested in giving up their lucrative positions to become government employees.

In order to ensure the participation of these merchant seamen, who were not interested in leaving their lucrative positions to become government employees, Congress gave private ships the legal right to attack and seize enemy vessels, and to keep a percentage of the spoils. Two types of commissions were authorized: The first was for privateers, whose sole mission was to seize enemy shipping; the other was letters of marque, which permitted the captain to engage in trade when possible and privateering when the opportunity arose.

During the 30 months that followed, civilian privateers captured so many ships and so much valuable cargo that British merchants brought pressure on their government to end the war. Baltimore alone docked 122 private armed vessels, and St. Michaels was another popular berth for privateers.

Each privateer captain was required to keep a journal and turn it over to the customs collector at his U.S. port of entry. Failure to do so resulted in a $1,000 fine and revocation of commission. In spite of the danger to their livelihood, some crossed the line into piracy. Captain Alexander Thompson of the *Midas* burned and sacked a plantation in Royal Island, Bahamas. Not long after the *Midas* put into port in North Carolina, news of the raid quickly reached President Monroe. Thompson was censured and lost his commission; he published a poetic rejoinder in the newspaper, which included these words:

To lend a hand in time of need When Britain she did burn Our Towns in every Part with speed. Determined to avenge the Cause I thought I would support the Laws And pay him [the British King] in his Kind.

[signed] The subject of the foregoing nonsense you may find at the sign of the 3 Living Squirrels, Fells Point Baltimore

A peace treaty signed on Christmas Eve 1814 ended Captain Thompson's censure – privateering was no longer allowed. He received his share of the considerable spoils he brought in and went on to command several trading vessels. He continued to reside at the Three Living Squirrels until his death in 1829.

St., 410/745-0100 or 877/466-0100, www.five gables.com, $150–425). It offers lodging and Aveda spa treatments, including herbal baths and massage. Spa services are additional, and spa package specials are available throughout the year.

Hambleton Inn (202 Cherry St., 410/745-3350 or 866/745-3350, www.hambletoninn.com, Apr.–Nov. $145–275, Dec.–Mar. $184–265) offers five rooms with private bath in a lovely 1860 Victorian. The inn is in the middle of St. Michaels, but is a quiet two blocks away from the main street, on the water. It's open year-round, and a dock slip is available for a nominal fee. Enclosed porches decorated with seasoned wicker furniture look out on the harbor.

Aida's Victoriana Inn (205 Cherry St., 410/745-3368 or 888/316-1282, www.victoriana inn.com, $149–279) is across the street from the Hambleton, with very similar ambience and facilities. It also offers seven rooms with full bath, and one room is pet-friendly.

$250 and Up

The fanciest place in town, the ◖ **Inn at Perry Cabin** (308 Watkins Ln., 410/745-2200 or 800/722-2949, www.perrycabin.com, $330–770), was originally the dwelling place of Samuel Hambleton, aide-de-camp to Commodore Oliver Hazard Perry in the War of 1812. When Hambleton retired to St. Michaels in 1816, he designed the north wing of the manor house to resemble Perry's cabin on the flagship *Niagara*—the ship that won the battle of Lake Erie. The property changed hands several times, and in 1989, the Greek Revival–style inn and surrounding property was bought and renovated by Sir Bernard Ashley (husband of Laura Ashley of chintz-and-prints fame). The inn features 78 guestrooms and suites, dockage, a heated indoor pool, health complex, helicopter access, and conference center, all set in protected wetlands and carefully tended gardens; the ambience is a cross between an upper-crust English country house and a top-level American hotel. There's even a snooker room and a secret passage in the library. Each of the rooms is spacious and varied in layout and feeling, individually decorated with antiques and compatible modern amenities in a simple, sleek style. Many have fireplaces and telescopes for viewing marsh wildlife. Expensive? Oh, yes. But prices include a full breakfast and afternoon tea in the inn's exceptional restaurant, and guests receive full value—the rooms and service are superb, and the inn is far enough from downtown St. Michaels to be a peaceful retreat, yet close enough to be easily accessible.

FOOD

An inexpensive place for breakfast, lunch, and dinner, **Chesapeake Cove** (204 S. Talbot, 410/745-3300, 11 A.M.–4 P.M. Mon.–Tues., 11 A.M.–8 P.M. Wed.–Fri., 8 A.M.–8 P.M. Sat., 8 A.M.–6 P.M. Sun., $8–20) is often crowded with locals.

Acme Markets (114 S. Talbot, 410/745-9819, 7 A.M.–9 P.M. daily) is a good place to pick up picnic fixings and household items.

A former clam-shucking shack, the **Crab Claw** (304 Mill St., Navy Point next to the Maritime Museum, 410/745-2900, www.the crabclaw.com, lunch and dinner daily Mar.–Nov., $20) is reputed to have the best steamed crab around, and it serves crab in every other conceivable form, too.

The ◖ **Sherwood's Landing** (in the Inn at Perry Cabin, 308 Watkins Ln., breakfast, lunch, tea, and dinner daily, breakfast $11, lunch $20, dinner $32, reservations required for dinner) is a wonderful splurge served in a chandelier-lit dining room. The menu and wine list reflect the continental leanings of Chef Mark Salter, who trained in Germany, Switzerland, and France before coming to Sir Bernard Ashley's Llangoed Hall Inn in Wales. The food is sophisticated and delicious—how about sweet chili–glazed veal short ribs and grilled jumbo shrimp on sautéed French beans with parsnip hash cake and crispy butternut squash chips ($34)?

INFORMATION

For local tourist information in St. Michaels, contact the **St. Michaels Business Association** (P.O. Box 1221, St. Michaels, MD 21663, 410/745-0411 or 800/808-7622, www.stmichaelsmd.org).

Tilghman Island

Pittsburgh Post-Gazette writer Jayne Clark once noted, "If St. Michaels appears perfectly coiffed, then its neighboring community of Tilghman Island hasn't shaved in a few days." Eighty percent of the 750 people who call Tilghman (TILman) home make their living as watermen. Of the 10–15 working skipjacks that remain in service on the Chesapeake, eight are moored on the island, in Dogwood Harbor. Several of these, along with larger boats, are available for charter.

RECREATION
Tours and Charter Boats
Wade Murphy (410/886-2176 or 410/829-3976) takes guests for two-hour pleasure cruises ($30) aboard the oldest skipjack under sail, the *Rebecca T. Ruark.* The *Rebecca* was built in 1886 and refuses to give in to age; she's won local skipjack races nine out of 10 times.

Captain Mike Richards (410/886-2215 or 800/690-5080, www.chesapeakelights.com) takes visitors out on the motor-powered **Sharpe's Island** for a cruise around five lighthouses on the Chesapeake Bay ($65) or a sunset cruise ($50). Longer trips are available by reservation. The captain also offers full- and half-day Chesapeake Lights Tours, a look at some or all of the bay's 10 lighthouses. Captain Chris Richards (800/690-5080) offers visitors a champagne sunset sail on the 45-foot 1935 Bay Ketch, **Lady Patty.**

Captain Bill Fish (yes!) operates **Nancy Ellen,** a bay boat finished off to yacht standards, and equipped with light tackle and fly fishing equipment.

ACCOMMODATIONS AND FOOD
Originally constructed in the 1920s as a fishing camp for vacationing anglers trying their luck at the Eastern Shore, the two-story **Sinclair House** (5718 Black Walnut Point Rd. 410/886-2147 or 888/859-2147, www.sinclairhouse.biz, $119–129) was converted into the island's first B&B and remains a historic landmark on Tilghman Island. Sinclair House's innkeepers have lived and worked

around the world. Monica, from Peru, met Jake in Guinea-Bissau, West Africa, where she served as an international officer with UNICEF and he was on diplomatic assignment to the U.S. Embassy. During their travels, both innkeepers were avid collectors of local art and handicrafts. Sinclair House now displays their eclectic treasures. Each of the four guestrooms (all have private baths) has a theme: African, Indonesian, Moroccan, and Peruvian. The inn closes during the winter.

Black Walnut Point Inn (end of Black Walnut Rd., 410/886-2452, www.blackwalnut point.com, $120–225) has four rooms in the main building and a cottage, all with private baths, tennis courts, and a pool on 57 acres. Rates at this upscale private resort on the tip of Tilghman Island require a two-night minimum on weekends.

The **Lazyjack Inn** (5907 Tilghman Island Rd., off Dogwood Harbor, 410/886-2215 or 800/690-5080, www.lazyjackinn,com, $129–176) is as quiet and tranquil as it gets. The 160-year-old house offers four rooms, each with private bath, and each with a special feature, such as a water view, fireplace, or private entrance. Mike and Carol Richards make a sumptuous breakfast to greet you in the sunny dining room overlooking the harbor. Mike also operates the *Lady Patty.*

The **❰ Bay Hundred** (6178 Tilghman Rd., 410/886-2126, lunch and dinner daily, $10–29), just north of the Knapps Narrows Bridge, is a casual place with great views and good food. Owner Fanoula Sullivan brings sophistication to the usual seafood-restaurant menu, featuring filet Chesapeake (beef mignon in bacon, topped with crabmeat) and salmon Rockefeller (grilled, topped with fresh sautéed spinach). The menu is broad and eclectic; reservations are essential.

INFORMATION
For updated local tourist information on Tilghman Island, visit www.tilghmanisland.com and click on "Welcome to Tilghman Island."

Oxford

Judging strictly from its decelerated pace of life, Oxford is tough to peg as one of two ports of entry for all of colonial Maryland (the other was Anne Arundel, later known as Annapolis). Before the Revolution, Oxford was a booming shipping and trade town; after the loss of British ships and the subsequent trade, the town dwindled. Following the Civil War, Oxford entered into a new period of prosperity thanks to the railroad and increasing national markets for local oysters. With the diminution of the oyster beds in the early 1900s, Oxford once again tightened down. Today, the town is mainly a home for watermen and a sleepy getaway for visitors—there's not a lot to do in Oxford, and most people like it that way.

SIGHTS
The Oxford Bellevue Ferry
The ferry (410/745-9023, www.oxfordbellevue ferry.com) has been in business since 1683, making it the oldest privately run ferry service in America. It crosses the Tred Avon River (0.75 mile), making 25–30 trips a day, and has counted Paul Newman and the prime minister of Madagascar among its passengers. The ferry runs 9 A.M.–sunset daily March 1–November. Drive or walk aboard: walk-on passengers pay $2, car and driver pay $8 one-way or $12 round-trip.

Oxford Historic Homes
Oxford has a number of buildings rich in the history of recent centuries. Most are private residences, so please enjoy them from the outside. **Oxford Custom House** (N. Morris St. and the Strand) created in 1976, is an exact replica of the first Federal Custom House built by Jeremiah Banning, the first Federal Collector of Customs. It's open weekends from April through late autumn. The **Academy House** (Bratt Mansion, 205 N. Morris St.) was the officers' residence for the Maryland Military Academy from 1848 to 1855. **Barnaby House** (212 N. Morris St.) was built in the 1770s by

Oxford Custom House

local captain Richard Barnaby. The **Grapevine House** (309 N. Morris St.) was built in 1798; the grapevine in front of the house was brought to Oxford from the Isle of Jersey in 1810.

Byberry and Calico are two houses moved to the grounds of **Cutts & Case** boatworks (306 Tilghman St.) in the 1930s. Byberry is Oxford's oldest house, dating from 1695. The original structure is a typical early Oxford cottage. Calico, a Tudor-style cottage, was built in the early 1700s. Cutts & Case is a family-owned business world-renowned for classic yacht design, construction, and restoration. Even those unfamiliar with wooden boats will recognize the shop's crossed-flags logo. The smell of shaved cedar fills the workshops, and beautiful wooden boats in all stages of restoration line the pier behind the buildings.

ACCOMMODATIONS AND FOOD
The Robert Morris Inn (314 N. Morris St. and the Strand, 410/226-5111 or

888/823-4012, www.robertmorrisinn.com, breakfast and lunch daily, dinner Thurs.–Mon. Apr.–Nov.) dates back to 1710, when it was put together by ships' carpenters—evident in the wooden pegged paneling in the formal dining room. Robert Morris Jr. ran the Oxford-based shipping business started by his father; the endeavor was so successful, Morris was able to lend large sums of money to finance the colonies' fight against Britain. He counted George Washington as a friend, and, after warming up his pen hand writing checks to the Continental Congress, became a signer of the Declaration of Independence, the Articles of Confederation, and the U.S. Constitution. From April to November (and some winter weekends), the inn offers simply decorated bed-and-breakfast rooms in the main building (private baths, $110–290). The establishment is celebrated for its traditional Chesapeake seafood and fine dining—more casual in the back tavern and formal in the front dining room ($25). Author James Michener, who spent considerable time here researching his book *Chesapeake,* claims the inn's crab cakes are the best: "Raise a glass of beer in memory of an old-timer who enjoyed the place very much," he said.

Robert Morris Inn also owns the **Sandaway Lodge,** a rambling Victorian half a block away on a private beach (many rooms have enclosed porches, $140–290). Since the Sandaway is used frequently for weddings, the leafy interior of the gigantic weeping beech tree on the grounds has seen its share of tipsy wedding guests.

C **Combsberry** (4837 Evergreen Rd., 410/226-5353, www.combsberry.com, $250–395) is just plain gorgeous, one of the premier historic homes on the Eastern Shore. The land was purchased in 1718 for 21,000 pounds of tobacco and 50 pounds of silver; the plantation's whitewashed brick manor house was built in 1730. After years of desultory care, the property was purchased by a group of investors for quick turnaround. Fortunately for visitors, the real estate market took a dive, and two of the partners, Mahmood and Ann Shariff, were reluctant to part with the property. They bought out their associates and restored the crumbling relic into an elegant, artistic guest house. Breakfast is served either in the formal dining room or in the country kitchen that overlooks the nine-acre grounds dotted with majestic magnolia and willow trees and informal gardens. Four guestrooms are in the main house, and two more are in a newly built carriage house. All have private baths and water views, and are decorated in English country style.

Also recommended in Oxford is the **Pier St. Restaurant and Marina** (W. Pier St., 410/226-5171, 11:30 A.M.–9 P.M. daily, $10 lunch, $20 dinner, closed during the winter), which serves an American menu strong on seafood.

INFORMATION

For local tourist information in Oxford, contact the **Oxford Business Association** (410/745-9023, www.portofoxford.com).

Easton

Easton almost has the look of a movie set—a handsome little town with unique, locally owned shops, an exceptional art museum, and carefully maintained homes. The county seat, Easton has been awarded the ongoing "Main Street" designation; and in 2000, it received recognition for excellence in the area of downtown revitalization set by the Maryland Main Street Program and the National Trust for His-

toric Preservation's National Main Street Center. If anything, it has more to offer visitors than ever. The message board at St. Andrew's Anglican Church in town advertises, "Broken hearts mended." What more could you ask?

SIGHTS
Academy of the Arts
The academy (106 South St., 410/822-2787,

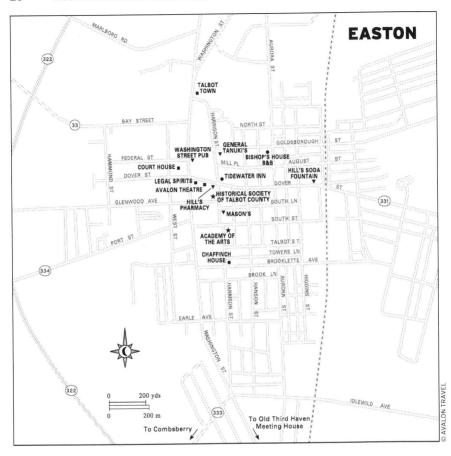

www.art-academy.org, 10 A.M.–4 P.M. Mon.–Sat., open until 8 P.M. Tues.–Thurs., closed Aug., $3 adults, $2 children over 12) is a modern space in an old building.

The facade is a restored 1820s schoolhouse, but the inside is all space and light. The academy serves two main purposes: a public arts program with sunny, well-equipped workshops, and a display space for professionally curated exhibits. The quality of any display space reflects its curators, and the hardworking staff at the academy chooses extremely well. The museum often partners with the National Gallery of Art in Washington, D.C., and was the recipient of the

Grover Batts Collection, 178 important works from artists such as Thomas Hart Benton and Rockwell Kent. Though the emphasis is on work by Eastern Shore residents, exhibitions include pieces by internationally acclaimed artists. A past exhibit focused on master Russian Impressionist Nikolai Timkov and his contemporaries. This work, though not widely known, was exceptional in every way. The permanent collection includes works by James McNeil Whistler, Grant Wood, Leonard Basking, and other notables.

Old Third Haven Meeting House

In 1682, a small group of Quakers took

© JOANNE MILLER

Easton Courthouse

two years to build what is now known as the meeting house (405 S. Washington St., 410/822-0293). The white clapboard building, still in use, is the oldest religious structure in the United States and the earliest dated building in Maryland. The meeting house stands in an open grove of trees at the end of a lane (look for the small sign on the west side of the street). It's almost always open, and in summer, you may see the resident family of fat woodchucks scurrying about. William Penn was among the prominent Quakers who sat in the simple wooden pews to worship; George Fox, founder of the Religious Society of Friends (Quakers) sent books to this meeting, establishing the first public library in the province. All are welcome to attend a meeting any Sunday at 10 A.M. (the brick building next to the meeting house is used in the winter).

ENTERTAINMENT AND RECREATION
Historical Society Tours
The Society (25 S. Washington St., 410/822-0773, www.hstc.org) offers several walking tours of the town to acquaint visitors with its many historic buildings. The South Washington Street offices house a permanent exhibit of local history (10 A.M.–4 P.M. Mon.–Sat., free) and operates **Tharpe Antiques & Decorative Arts** (30 S. Washington St.) as a museum shop. The Historical Society's "The Craftsmen and the Collector Tour" is a 45-minute guided tour of three houses that represent each of the three centuries since the founding of Talbot County in 1662—"Ending of Controversie" is a faithful reproduction of the 1670 home of Quaker Wenlock Christison. The Joseph Neall House was the residence and shop of a Quaker craftsman of the late 18th century, and the James Neall House (1810) was built in the federal style for a family of 11, plus retainers.

The Historical Society also offers a Frederick Douglass Driving Tour that includes 14 sites connected to the abolitionist, including his birthplace. Ask for a brochure at the offices or by phone.

Avalon Theatre
The theater (40 East Dover St., 410/822-7299,

www.avalontheatre.com) presents lively year-round entertainment, including movies, choirs, musicians from the Caribbean and New Orleans, and ornate displays (one year, model trains and railroad lore filled the space at Christmas). The real star, though, is the restored art deco theater itself, with its state-of-the-art sound and lighting systems. Call for the schedule.

Pickering Creek Audubon Center

This is a private sanctuary operated by the Audubon Society (11450 Audubon Ln., 410/822-4903, www.pickeringcreek.org, 8:30 A.M.–5 P.M. Mon.–Fri., 10 A.M.–4 P.M. Sat., donations appreciated). The buildings are closed on Sunday, but the grounds are open to visitors. The property—the home of a Matapeake Indian village prior to European colonization—features more than 100 acres of hardwood forest, including old-growth oak, beech, and hickory, and 270 acres under low-impact cultivation (an organic community garden). Additional acreage is in conservation easements, buffer strips, wildlife plantings (where local farmers plant a certain portion of the land in feed for wildlife), and a nature preserve. There's a mile of shoreline, and fresh and brackish marshes on the Wye River. The thrust here is on education, and the center offers numerous opportunities to enjoy the outdoors and learn. Evening canoe trips, forest ecology walks, herb workshops, and sea kayaking are a few of the one- and two-day programs that take place throughout the warmer months.

There's a nature walk, and the sanctuary is studded with more than 40 bluebird boxes—as you might expect of the Audubon Society, this is an excellent bird-watching location. To get there, take Route 662 north from Easton (this runs parallel with U.S. 50) past the Easton Airport. Follow the signs: Turn left at Sharp Road (west), and veer right at the Y. Turn right (north) to Presquille Road, then right on Audubon Lane.

SHOPPING

Harrison Street in Easton is the site of several antiques and collectibles shops. Contemporary crafts and clothing shops also line the street. **Talbot Town** (218 N. Washington St.), a small in-town mall, features a Talbots (no relation) and several upscale home decorating shops. **Courthouse Square Shops** line a pass-through from Harrison Street to Washington Street; of note is **Rowens Stationery Store,** featuring local-interest books as well as bestsellers.

There are several antique shops and multi-dealer shops in the 7700 and 7800 blocks of **Ocean Gateway** (Rte. 50). **Foxwell's** (7793 Ocean Gateway) and **Camelot Antiques** (7871 Ocean Gateway) are representative. The **Wood Duck** (8374 Ocean Gateway) is a gallery featuring decoys, carvings, limited editions, and original artwork. Also check out **Sullivan's Antiques Warehouse** (28272 St. Michaels Rd./Rte. 33).

A favorite **"nameless" store** is at the intersection of Royal Oak Road and Bellevue Ferry Road. Two old buildings stand across from one another—one has furniture piled end over end, and the other has everything else. Great prices and great fun.

ACCOMMODATIONS

The **Tidewater Inn** (101 E. Dover St., 410/822-1300 or 800/237-8775, www.tidewaterinn.com, room $109–269, suite $300) combines the intimate feel of a B&B with the amenities of a large hotel. Once a haunt of camouflage-coated goose hunters, the inn caters to upscale customers today (the goose hunters are still there, but now they dress for dinner). It's not as formal as it sounds, but leave the muddy boots and dogs outside. They're tough on the carpet and mahogany antiques in the lobby—and they'll wreak havoc in the pool. This is the best "modern" hotel in the area. It offers special-rate packages throughout the year, and there's a sophisticated restaurant on the premises (brunch 10 A.M.–4 P.M. Sat.–Sun., lunch 11 A.M.–4 P.M. Mon. and Thurs.–Fri., dinner 4 P.M.–10 P.M. Thurs.–Mon., $9–30). The **Decanter Wine Room** features more than 2,000 wine selections.

If an 1893 Queen Anne Victorian is more to your taste, try **Chaffinch House** (132 S.

Harrison St., 410/822-5074 or 800/861-5074, $140–180). All of the rooms have private baths and are decorated in period style.

Also recommended is the **Bishop's House B&B** (214 Goldsborough St., 410/820-7290 or 800/223-7290, www.bishophouse.com, $180–190).

FOOD

◖ Mason's (22 S. Harrison St., 410/822-3204, www.masonsgourmet.com, lunch and dinner daily, $8–32) is a charming place to stop for a delicious gourmet lunch or dinner (try the rockfish tournado stuffed with local crab, $28), followed by handmade chocolates. It was noted by *Wine Spectator* magazine as one of the "best restaurants in the world for wine lovers."

Hill's Soda Fountain, in Hill's Drug Stores (32 E. Dover St., 410/822-2666, store open 8 A.M.–7 P.M. Mon.–Sat., fountain open 8 A.M.–4 P.M. Mon.–Fri., 8 A.M.–3 P.M. Sat., closed Sun., $7) is the real thing. You'll find malts and burgers, tuna sandwiches, and chips.

General Tanuki's (25 Goldsborough St., 410/819-0707, lunch, and dinner Mon.–Sat., dinner Sun., $9–25) features an eclectic menu with a pan-Asian influence. Lunch sandwiches include the "Thanksgiving": smoked turkey and wild mushroom stuffing with orange chili sauce on marble rye ($10), and the dinner menu features Hawaiian pizzas ($10) and Thai mussels ($19).

Legal Spirits Tavern (42 East Dover St., 410/820-0765, lunch and dinner daily, lunch $9, dinner $22) offers Eastern Shore cuisine—cream of crab soup is a specialty—complete with copious desserts.

One of the local happening hot spots at night is the **Washington Street Pub,** across from the courthouse (20 N. Washington, 410/822-9011, www.wstpub.com, lunch and dinner daily, $7–18). It has a raw bar and 19 of the coldest beers in town on tap.

INFORMATION

For updates on Easton, contact the **Easton Business Management Association** (410/822-0065, www.eastonmd.org).

Greater Talbot County

The flotilla of pleasure boats that plies the 600-plus miles of Talbot County's coastline might fool visitors into thinking that maritime-related tourism is the county's most important product—but it's not. Although Talbot County has the longest shoreline of any county in the United States, agriculture still ranks first as the largest local commercial industry, a fact easily proven by a short drive away from the well-known haunts of captains and crews. Soybeans, corn, and wheat make up the bulk of the produce that serves as the backbone of Talbot's economy. All told, farms in the region gross more than $40 million a year. However, the waters—including the Tred Avon, Tuckahoe, Wye, Miles, and Choptank Rivers—produce their own riches, from seafood to dockage. This is a difficult place to visit on a tight budget, so be prepared.

Talbot County Scenic Loop

There's a 25-mile scenic loop from St. Michaels, ideal for drivers or bicyclists: Drive east on Route 33 to Bellevue Road, then make a left (south) on Bellevue to the ferry. Float across to Oxford, then take Route 333 (Almshouse Rd.) east, then north, connecting with Route 322 to Easton. Return on Route 33 to St. Michaels.

Information

An overview of all the towns in Talbot county and their attractions can be obtained from the **Talbot County Office of Tourism** (11 S. Harrison St., Easton, MD 21601, 410/770-8000, www.tourtalbot.org/visitorinformation).

CAMBRIDGE

Cambridge, the largest town in the county, is one of the oldest in the state, settled in 1684.

Tobacco built the local economy on the backs of slaves. As trading ships from Europe began to dock in Cambridge during the 1700s (the unusable harbor had been dredged out to create a deepwater port), seafood and muskrat pelts joined tobacco as the major exports. The industrial revolution brought lumber mills and flour mills to Cambridge, and in the late 1800s, oyster-packing became the major source of employment, second only to Baltimore. In 1911, Phillips Packing Company took over the oyster packing plant, and drove the town to new heights of prosperity, earning the name "Queen City." Phillips folded in the 1950s, and Cambridge was left to struggle.

Museums

The city of Cambridge merged two small museums focusing on different aspects of maritime history into a $10 million showplace maritime museum on the water. The former James B. Richardson Maritime Museum added its collections to The **Brannock Maritime Museum** (106 Hayward St., 410/228-6938, projected opening spring 2008) to create detailed displays on shipbuilding, oystering, and Dorchester County's role in American history. Call Dorchester County Tourism (41//228-1000 or 800/522-8687) for a progress update and visitor information.

The **Meredith House and Nield Museum** (902 LaGrange Ave. at Maryland Ave., 410/228-7953, 10 A.M.–3 P.M. Tues.–Sat. April–Nov., 10 A.M.–1 P.M. Tues.–Fri. and 11 A.M.–3 P.M. Sat. Dec.–March, $3 adults) is the 1760 Georgian home of a former Maryland Governor; period antiques and a doll and toy collection are on display. The museum features antique toys, agricultural and maritime artifacts, Native American handiwork, a blacksmith shop, and a colonial herb garden.

The **Harriet Tubman Museum and Learning Center** (424 Race St., Cambridge, 410/228-0401, tours by request) stocks a few items, but more significantly houses a learning center focusing on the life of Dorchester-born national heroine Harriet Tubman. Storyboards line the walls, illuminating the life of Tubman

and other famous black Americans, the Underground Railroad, and other topics of interest. Admission is free, but donations are appreciated. **Hometown Tours** works out of the gift shop, and offers a tour of the county centered on the life and times of Ms. Tubman ($10 adults, $7 kids). Other tours—with an African American viewpoint—can be tailored to individual interests and may include historic buildings and churches.

Dorchester Arts Center (DAC)

This local art hot spot (120 High St., Cambridge, 410/228-7782, www.tourdorchester .org, 10 A.M.–2 P.M. Mon.–Sat., 1–4 P.M. Sun., free) offers classes in artistic disciplines and exhibits local work. The gift shop is inspired and well worth a stop. The location, in a stately Victorian, is another reason to visit High Street. DAC is redeveloping the historic Nathan Building at 321 High Street and plans to expand classes and gallery space to that location.

Cambridge Historic Homes

During Cambridge's wealthiest periods, **High Street** was *the* address, and a stroll from the long wharf up to Poplar Street provides the evidence. Several Maryland governors had homes on High, and the properties have been cherished and kept up over the years. Homes range in age from the late 18th century to the early 20th, most built 1850–1880. A few of note are the **home of Governor Charles Goldsborough** (200 High St.), built in 1790; it's one of the best-preserved federal-style houses on the Eastern Shore. The **Sulivane House** (205 High St.) was built in 1763 and was home to generations of Sulivanes, including Colonel Clement Sulivane, a Confederate solider who participated in the burning of Richmond. The **Bayly House** (207 High St.) was built in 1755 in Annapolis and barged across the bay in 1760—still in the Bayly family, the white-columned porches recall the old South. **Christ Episcopal Church,** on the corner of High and Church Streets, was built from stones shipped over as ballast—there's no natural building stone in the area. The grave-

High Street mansion in Cambridge

yard was established before the Revolutionary War; Civil War era graves of both Confederate and Union boys lie next to one another. The Dorchester County Department of Tourism publishes an excellent free guide to historic homes in Cambridge, including those on High Street. Visitors can pick one up at the Arts Center. For an interesting contrast, you might want to walk up Water Street and stroll on Vue de Leau Street, one block away from High Street; these were the homes of local watermen.

Shopping

Cambridge has a dandy antiques center, **Packing House Antiques** (411A Dorchester Ave.), plus nearby **Bay County Antiques** (415 Dorchester Ave.). Both renovated warehouses (at the intersection of Dorchester and Washington Sts.) offer miles of aisles and multiple dealers. The 400–800 blocks of Race Street also feature a variety of shops.

Recreation

Boat tours are a popular way to see the area.

The **Cambridge Lady** (410/221-0776) is a classic wooden yacht that offers several tours, including "Michener's Chesapeake Tour," which visits Oxford and Cambridge by water and includes narration that brings the times and places of the novel to life. Combination walking and boat tours, a nautical history tour, and eco-tours are also offered, along with a cruise-and-dine option (you're ferried to a local restaurant) or dine-aboard buffets. Co-captains Frank and Sherri Herbert are locals who love the area and freely share their enthusiasm. The *Lady* sails daily May–October (Nov.–Apr., they head down to Florida). If a skipjack is more your style, the **Nathan of Dorchester** (410/228-7141, www.skipjack-nathan.org) is the boat for you. The *Nathan* is newish—built in 1994—but has all the fine features of traditional skipjacks. Trips include narration on the lives of Chesapeake Bay watermen. The *Nathan* sails most Saturdays May–October. Both boats are docked in Cambridge.

For sportfishing charters, the **Joint Venture** (311 Nathan Ave., Cambridge 410/228-7837), under Captain Ben Parks, provides a variety of bottom fishing, trolling, and casting day trips, from Tilghman Island to the Virginia line.

Accommodations

The ❰ **Cambridge House** (112 High St., Cambridge, 410/221-7700 or 877/221-7799, www.cambridgehousebandb.com, $125–175), a bed-and-breakfast, is an elegant Queen Anne–style Victorian built for a wealthy sea captain. It was a peeling wreck when innkeeper Stuart Schefers took over in 1996—now, the meticulously renovated rooms are decorated in period antiques and all have fireplaces, private bath, air-conditioning, and TV. Stuart, a professional restaurateur, opened 37 restaurants in New York City before retiring to Cambridge. The breakfasts are spectacular, as you might expect.

Another bed-and-breakfast, the **Mill Street Inn** (114 Mill St., Cambridge, 410/901-9144, www.millstinn.com, $125–225) is in a beautifully refurbished Victorian that opened for business in 2006. The innkeepers, Skip and Jennie, are retired teachers and organic farmers who serve up a lovely breakfast and tea. Each of the three suites is beyond comfortable; prices reflect day of the week and season (midweek and off-season are always lowest). This is an adults-only, no-pets inn.

Luxury, thy name is ❰ **Hyatt Regency Chesapeake Bay** (100 Heron Blvd., 410/901-1234, $170 and up). This painstakingly designed and landscaped spa resort is a feast for the eye (and stomach). Perched like a castle on the shores of the Choptank River, it offers an 18-hole, par-71 golf course (the River Marsh Golf Club, created by Keith Foster); a full-service, top-flight spa (the Stillwater); tennis courts; a small private beach with paddleboats; a marina (with a provisions store); an exercise facility with classes; and three swimming pools, one of which appears to merge with the river below it. Visitors pull up to the grand circular arrival court via a private entry road that winds through natural plantings and the golf course. Every room has a view—of the river, fountains, or the golf course—in this truly beautiful

place. Guests who choose not to dawdle in their airy and spacious rooms can mingle with others in the handsome glass-enclosed bar or Michener's Library, shoot a game of snooker, or just sit by the big outdoor fireplace at night and roast a s'more. Though the resort appears to be a playground for adults, families are equally welcome; Hyatt offers Camp Hyatt at Pirate's Cove, activities for children ages 4–12 (half-day sessions $28, full days $52).

Luxury has its price, as the room rates indicate. Use of the beach, pools and tennis courts is included with the room, but exercise classes, golf, and spa treatments are extra (expect to pay $100–200 for spa services).

Food

The ❰ **Portside** (201 Trenton St., Cambridge, 410/228-9007, lunch and dinner Tues.–Sun., $5–20) is the sort of ultracasual place where locals come for a bite. The menu focuses on seafood as entrées, in sandwiches, and in baskets with fries. There's a good view of the boats plying the river below. Also recommended in Cambridge is **Snappers** (112 Commerce St., 410/228-0112, 11 A.M.–10 P.M. Mon.–Sat., 11 A.M.–9 P.M. Sun.), another local favorite for seafood.

For a more upscale, fine dining experience, you'll have plenty to choose from. The latest addition to Cambridge's best restaurants is the **Blue Point Provision Company** (100 Heron Blvd., in the Hyatt Chesapeake, 410/901-1234, dinner daily, $30). A seafood specialty eatery, it's located at the far end of the resort, looking out over the River Marsh Marina on the shores of the Choptank River. Panoramic water views and an outdoor patio make this an outstanding place to view the sunset over the Chesapeake. Reservations recommended.

The soaring ceiling and subtle lighting of ❰ **Water's Edge Grill** (100 Heron Blvd., in the Hyatt Chesapeake, 410/901-1234, breakfast, lunch, and dinner daily, $10–35) reflect the lofty aims of the chefs at what is undoubtedly the most elegant restaurant in this part of the bay. Sophisticated variations on regional specialties such as crab cakes and roast duck are well prepared and beautifully presented.

Also in the Hyatt Chesapeake, the **Eagle's Nest Bar and Grille** (100 Heron Blvd., 410/901-1234, 11 A.M.–3:30 P.M. daily, $12) may be the most manly golf club restaurant and bar ever conceived. Large bronze sculptures of Chesapeake wildlife by William Turner stand guard over a long, dark-toned wood room with enormous windows and imposing wrought-iron chandeliers. It's open for beer, cocktails, and sandwiches.

Greater Dorchester County

Dorchester is largely rural and threaded by rivers, including the 68-mile Choptank, immortalized by authors James Michener *(Chesapeake)* and John Barth *(Tidewater Tales* and *Floating Opera).*

Tourism is breathing new life into the city and the county. In addition to time-honored boating recreation, **Sailwinds Park,** a $30 million waterfront multi-use facility for concerts, fairs, festivals, and trade shows, is under development in Cambridge; a beautifully designed Hyatt golf resort and spa has opened; a Holiday Inn Express has set down roots; and other major players in the hospitality industry will surely follow.

Spocott Windmill

Those interested in machines and history will want to stop by this structure on Route 343, six miles west of Cambridge in the vicinity of Lloyds. This is a rare post-style mill (it sits aloft a four-foot-diameter, 200-year-old stripped white oak tree like a lollipop on a stick). Though the interior is seldom open to the public, it's worth a look. At one time, 18 post windmills operated in Dorchester County—all were eventually destroyed by forces of nature. The Spocott was destroyed in the blizzard of 1880 and rebuilt in 1971, using the original millstones, interior stairs, and much of the original timber.

RECREATION
◖ Islands and Towns Tour

This 85-mile road trip begins and ends in Cambridge. The route makes a big loop around Dorchester County, swinging past several historic towns, crossing a large wildlife refuge and wandering into two island communities. None of these "attractions" are developed, in the tourist sense, so be prepared for some serene country vistas and great history. Since some of the route is on major highways, it's not recommended for cyclists. All distances are approximate.

Leave Cambridge heading east on U.S. 50, and turn left (north) on Route 16 (three miles east of town). Follow Route 16 five miles to the village of **East New Market,** settled in the mid-1600s. Most of the extant Colonial-era houses are along Route 16 (which veers to the left at Linkwood Rd.) and the intersection of Route 14 (Rte. 14 loops around to the town of **Secretary** and the Suicide Bridge Restaurant. The village that makes up the historic district is bounded on the south and east by Route 392 and on the west by Creamery Road. It features 75 buildings representing architecture from the 18th, 19th, and 20th centuries. The buildings are privately owned, and most look nearly new. For detailed information on some of the more prominent houses, contact **Dorchester County Tourism** (800/522-TOUR, www.tourdorchester.org) and ask for the *East New Market Brochure.*

Take Route 14 east and south out of town for five miles to Route 331, and follow it for six miles to **Vienna,** 0.5 mile below the intersection of U.S. 50. Settled about the same time as East New Market, Vienna's original name was "Vinnacokasimmon," after a native chief. It was also named Baltimore for a short period of time, at the request of the Calverts. Vienna prospered in the early years as a center for the tobacco trade and shipbuilding. As technology changed (and the river silted up), the town turned its focus away from industry and became a quiet residential village. It supports a B&B or two and a few antiques stores. As with East New Market, details on the town's architectural treasures (mostly on Water St. on the Nanticoke River, and on Church St. at the south end of Water St.) are in the brochure available from Dorchester County Tourism.

Leave Vienna and travel south on Crossroads Road six miles to Henry's Crossroads. Go right on Henry's Crossroads (west) to the end (two miles), and turn left (south) onto Griffith Neck Road, which turns into Bestpitch Ferry Road, to **Bucktown** (10 miles). Bucktown is the home of the former Brodess Plantation, birthplace of Harriet Tubman. Take Greenbrier Road three miles west to Maple Dam Road. Make a left (south) to Key Wallace Drive and the settlement of Seward.

Continue west on Key Wallace Drive through the top of **Blackwater National Wildlife Refuge** (three miles). As an alternative route, consider taking the refuge's driving tour, also great for cycling. Both routes dead-end on Church Creek Road.

Turn left on Church Creek/Golden Hill Road (south) until it dead-ends at Route 335/336, four miles. Turn right on Route 335/Hooper Island Road and follow it as far down into **Hooper Island** as you'd like (2–14 miles). You'll pass the diminutive Star of the Sea Chapel on the north side of the road; it was built before 1767 as a place of worship for local Roman Catholics. Hooper Island is actually a chain of islands named for the family that settled there in the late 1600s; Colonel Henry Hooper and his son, Brigadier General Henry Hooper, commanded local militias against the British during the Revolution. Nearly 75 years later, Ella Carroll—feminist, friend of Abraham Lincoln, and Northern spy—called the island home. Today, the dwellings are almost entirely made up of the homes of watermen, set among marshes—a surreal, floating landscape. Sandy's is a good place to stop for a snack and an opportunity to pick up a locally made souvenir.

church on Taylors Island

Return on Route 335 to Smithville Road and make a left (north) for seven miles until it dead-ends at Taylors Island Road (Rte. 16). Make a left, and within a mile, you'll be in the community of **Taylors Island.** This quiet village was settled in the 1650s. Along with late-18th-century churches and schools, it boasts a British ship's cannon captured by local militia during the War of 1812.

Return on Taylors Island Road east to Church Creek (five miles). **Old Trinity Church** (1716 Taylors Island Rd.) is worth a look. The chapel was built between 1675 and 1690, then later refurbished to its original state. The floor tiles (laid with a mortar of burnt oyster shells), altar table, and exterior brick walls are all original. Fifteen high-backed, gated pews made of beeswax-rubbed heart of pine, finished with handmade H-hinges, are faithful representations of the period. The loft in back was for slaves and servants, who were locked in during the service. The church still maintains an active (voluntary) congregation; services are at 11 A.M. on Sunday. Call the rectory

(410/228-2940) to set up a tour of the church, or wander about the old graveyard. A church regular commented that the headstones reflect the leading preoccupations of many Eastern Shore dwellers: boats, booze, and broads. You'll find all kinds of history here.

Route 16 will take you east and north back to Cambridge (five miles).

Blackwater National Wildlife Refuge

Once a farm used by muskrat trappers for the fur trade, the refuge was established in 1933 to provide sanctuary for migrating waterfowl (2145 Key Wallace Dr., Cambridge, MD 21613, 410/228-2677; Fish and Wildlife Service, 800/344-WILD, www.fws.gov/blackwater, visitors center 8 A.M.–4 P.M. Mon.–Fri., 9 A.M.– 5 P.M. Sat.–Sun. year-round). A daily permit is required: private vehicles cost $3 and pedestrian or bicyclists cost $1. Golden Eagle passes are accepted.

In the refuge, geese number approximately 35,000 and ducks exceed 15,000 at the peak of fall migration, usually in November. October–March is the best time to visit to see migratory birds, though many songbirds, reptiles, and mammals stay year-round. Blackwater is also a haven for three endangered or threatened species, the bald eagle (largest nesting population north of Florida), peregrine falcon, and Delmarva fox squirrel. The refuge is stunningly beautiful, particularly in the late afternoon when the setting sun reflects off the mirrored ponds and birds swoop to feed on the plentiful insects.

Blackwater may be seen in several different ways. The visitors center offers exhibits, naturalist talks, and films. From there, several walking trails, including a wheelchair-accessible loop, meander through different habitats. A wildlife drive along either a 6.5-mile loop or a 3.5-mile all-weather road winds along through ponds, woods, fields, and marshes; walking and biking on the wildlife drive are permitted. Cyclists may choose from a 20-mile loop or a 25-mile loop. Boaters may enter the refuge via one of the surrounding waterways April 1–September 30, but may not launch within the refuge (there is a public boat launch on Shorters Wharf Road on the southern boundary of the refuge).

Boat Tours

Let's say you were deeply influenced by *Showboat* in your youth—you'd probably like to checkout **Dorothy-Megan** (410/943-4775), run by the Choptank Riverboat Company in Hurlock. It's an 80-foot paddle-wheeler that offers sightseeing and lunch and dinner cruises late spring–October.

Sportfishing Charters

Sawyer Fishing Charters (1345 Hoopers Island Rd., Church Creek, 410/397-3743) will take you out into the bay to reel in the striped bass of your dreams. They offer full- and half-day trips, and special rates during the summer.

Bicycling

Dorchester County, like much of the Eastern Shore, is great biking territory. Along with the scenic loops in the Blackwater Refuge, an additional 32-mile back-road loop begins in Vienna. It covers part of the driving tour, but spends far more time on little-used roads. Take Crossroads Road south out of Vienna, and turn right (west) on Steels Neck Road. Continue to go straight when the road becomes New Bridge Road. It will dead-end at Ravenwood Road Turn left (south). Turn right at Drawbridge Road then left (west) on Decoursey Bridge Road. It dead-ends at Bucktown Road/Bestpitch Ferry Road Turn left (south). The turnoff for Greenbrier Road and Blackwater Refuge comes up about a mile down the road—if you take the short refuge loop on Key Wallace Dr., it will add another 12 miles to the trip. If you choose to continue south on Bucktown Road/ Bestpitch Ferry Road, it will turn into Griffith Neck Road (east), and turn sharply north (you'll cross the drawbridge). Continue on Drawbridge Road north to Steels Neck Road, and make a right (east) to retrace your path to Vienna.

ACCOMMODATIONS

The Tavern House (111 Water St., Vienna, 410/376-3347, $70–80) was built on the Nanticoke River as a combination pub-and-inn to serve travelers during colonial times. Today, it offers three simply decorated bedrooms, all with shared bath; two of the bedrooms have fireplaces.

FOOD

Old Salty's (2560 Hoopers Island Rd., Hoopers Island, 410/397-3752, 11 A.M.–6 P.M. daily, sandwiches $4–8, entrées $6–18) is an inexpensive place to stop for a sandwich or an entrée. The crab sandwiches and fresh fish sandwiches are quite good. Old Salty's has gained quite a reputation with visitors over the past few years, and not just for the cheap snacks. A big room next to the restaurant sells craft items made by local people. How could you resist a gold-painted crab shell filled with cotton snow, a glittering miniature Christmas tree and bear, especially when the bear is hoisting a jug to his snout? I couldn't—it has a place of honor on my tree. The woven potholders are also irresistible; anything for sale there shames made-in-Taiwan, just-for-tourists merchandise.

Suicide Bridge Restaurant (6304 Suicide Bridge Rd., Hurlock, 410/943-4689, mid-April–Dec., lunch and dinner Tues.–Sun., sandwiches $8, entrées $12–32) is the most popular eatery around with both locals and visitors. It's about 10 miles out of Cambridge, on the Choptank River. Again, the focus is on seafood, baked, boiled, broiled, or fried, but they also have a complete beef/chicken/veal selection. The atmosphere is boating casual (*good* shorts and collared knit shirt).

INFORMATION

For brochures and information updates, contact the **Dorchester County Department of Tourism** (visitors center, Tailwinds Park, east end of Rte. 50 Bridge, 410/228-1000 or 800/522-8687, www.tourdorchester.org, 8:30 A.M.–5 P.M. daily). You can't miss the 100-foot-tall soaring "sails" of Tailwinds Park-it's become an eastern shore landmark, and the symbol of a town that is determined to make itself into a top tourist destination.

SUICIDE BRIDGE

In case you're wondering why they call the short span that crosses a tributary of the Choptank River "Suicide Bridge," here's the story. Apparently, this bit of wood and concrete has all the allure of San Francisco's Golden Gate Bridge. What it lacks is height, being only 10-15 feet above the water. That didn't stop the bridge's first victim, a postmaster from Hurlock, who shot himself and fell into the creek. The second victim, a local farmer, followed suit. The third victim either jumped off the bridge and struck his head on a piling or was a victim of foul play – it was never determined.

The original structure was built in 1888, then replaced in 1910 and once again in 1968. Less than six months after the newest bridge was built, a longtime employee of Continental Can in Hurlock chose to end his life rather than return to work from his vacation. He jumped off the bridge and drowned. Not long after that, another man who was born and raised within half a mile of the bridge and who had moved away for several years came back and shot himself – on Suicide Bridge.

But things may be looking up for the unfortunate span: One woman who had jumped into the icy waters recently changed her mind and began calling for help. She was rescued by Dave Nickerson, who lives next to the creek (and owns a nearby restaurant). Local resident Pete Moxey says, "I don't think the bridge is jinxed. Maybe it's just the name that brings them here." The only way to guarantee peace on Suicide Bridge may be to rename it – how about "Second Thoughts Bridge?"

If you're on the Eastern Shore, keep an eye out for the **Tidewater Times,** a little (3.5 by 5 inches) powerhouse of a monthly publication that has lots of great information and articles about the Eastern Shore, especially Talbot and Dorchester counties. You can also find the *Times* online at www.tidewatertimes.com.

Salisbury

Salisbury, the largest city on the Eastern Shore (granted, Ocean City's population waxes and wanes seasonally), began as a mill community in the center of dense woods in 1732. The Wicomico River provided critical water access to the Chesapeake, and Salisbury grew as the principal crossroads of the southern Delmarva Peninsula.

The town of Salisbury burned to the ground in 1860 and was entirely rebuilt. Today, the town continues to thrive as a center of commerce, and offers major historical and recreational activities for visitors (and the restaurants are good, too).

SIGHTS
◖ Ward Museum of Wildfowl Art

What was once necessity has become art, and nowhere is this better demonstrated than at the Ward Museum of Wildfowl Art (909 S. Schumaker Dr., Salisbury, 410/742-4988, www .wardmuseum.org, 10 A.M.–5 P.M. Mon.–Sat.,

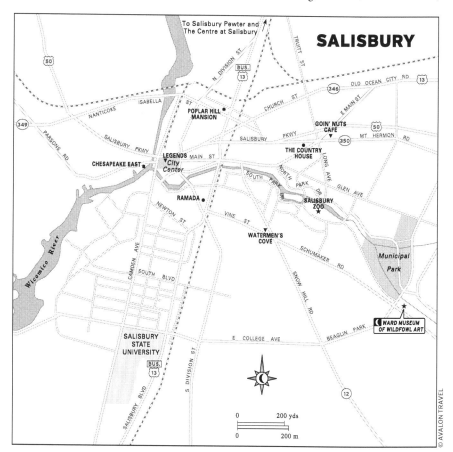

STOOL PIGEONS AND GUNNERS

In the 19th century, hunters gauged their success by the number of kills. The term "stool pigeon," which today alludes to someone who informs on his associates, originally referred to live passenger pigeons tethered to a tree-like post. Pigeons on the wing, being social creatures, would spiral down to land beside their brothers and be picked off by the hunter's guns. A good hunter with a repeating rifle could bring down 100 birds a day.

Once copious enough to darken the sky, the passenger pigeon population was endangered by the 1890s and extinct by 1914. Though it was too late for the gregarious passenger pigeon, Migratory Bird Laws were first passed in 1914, outlawing specific types of hunting. In 1918, the Migratory Bird Treaty prohibited commercial sale of game birds.

Chesapeake Bay Gunning Clubs, which started out in the 1850s, popularized the sport-hunting lifestyle, along with working companion dogs such as the Chesapeake Bay retriever and the Labrador and golden retrievers. Today, the clubs work actively to make sure the fate of the passenger pigeon isn't repeated. Through financial support and environmental lobbying, the clubs are largely responsible for the resurgence of waterfowl populations and habitat preservation on the Chesapeake.

noon–5 P.M. Sun., $9 adults, less for seniors and children). You will have to remind yourself that you are looking at carved and painted wood, not wild birds in flight. The work is extraordinary, as you might expect from the premier collection of wildfowl art in the world. The museum looks at the history and heritage of the art, from antique working decoys to contemporary carvings, and two additional galleries feature changing exhibits. Winners in all categories from the annual world competition are displayed, including Shootin' Stool (active decoys), Miniatures, and Decorative Lifesize. Among the winners of past Decorative Lifesize awards were "Road Kill Pheasant" (Winner, Best in the World—not only for the outrageously beautiful carving, but also for the sly humor), a pair of fighting cocks, and courting kestrels in midflight. Wow.

The exhibits have expanded to include jewelry and carved wood in a variety of diverse subjects, such as free-form sculptures, exotic plants, and other objects.

Salisbury Zoo

This little haven is a zoo hater's zoo (5 Park Dr., in Salisbury city park, 410/548-3188, www.salisburyzoo.org, 8 A.M.–7:30 P.M. daily Memorial Day–Labor Day, 8 A.M.–4:30 P.M. daily Labor Day–Memorial Day, free). Dr. Theodore Reed, Director Emeritus of the National Zoo, called it "one of the finest small zoos in North America," and so it is. Nearly 400 species—all native to the Americas—inhabit a compact and neatly landscaped 12 acres. One thing that makes this zoo unusual is the preponderance of natural habitats—cages are few. Bright colored macaws zoom around the tall trees, unhampered by wire; ducks and other waterfowl come and go at will on the stretch of Wicomico River that borders the zoo; prairie dogs tumble around their specially built enclosure. It's a peaceful place for a stroll and a special place for children.

Historic Sights

Salisbury has a major force for historical preservation in the Wicomico Historical Society (410/860-0447). The society maintains a small museum and store at **Pemberton Historical Park** (Pemberton Dr., 410/548-4900, www.pembertonpark.org), site of Pemberton Hall, built in 1741 for Colonel Isaac Handy. The grounds are threaded by 4.5 miles of self-guided nature trails, and the manor house may be toured 2–4 P.M. Sunday May–October and by appointment; a small fee is charged. Pemberton Historical Park hosts a number of special events during the year, notably the Colonial Fair (see the *Festivals and Events* section in this chapter). To get there from U.S. 50 east of Salisbury, turn left on Nanticoke Road, then take the first left on Pemberton Drive (south). Follow Pemberton Drive two miles; the park is on the left.

The historical society also publishes a walking tour of "Newtown"—now the oldest neighborhood in Salisbury—the area that was built immediately after the great fires of 1860 and 1886 destroyed much of the city (call 410/860-0447 for the brochure). One of the homes spared by the fires welcomes visitors: **Poplar Hill Mansion** (117 Elizabeth St., 410/749-1776, donations appreciated), built in 1799. It's open to the public for free tours 1–4 P.M. on the first and third Sunday of each month (tours arranged by appointment during other times, $3), and is a popular site for meetings and events.

The **Mason-Dixon Marker** lies north of Salisbury on the Delaware border, U.S. 13 just past Route 54 on the west side of the road. Charles Mason and Jeremiah Dixon surveyed the line between 1763 and 1767, and it was used as the formal dividing line between slave and free states. Maryland—below the Mason-Dixon Line—chose to be a free state, at least technically. One deciding factor was that the Emancipation Proclamation freed slaves only in those states that seceded from the Union. Therefore, slave owners in Maryland were not obligated by law to manumit their slaves.

SHOPPING

Between Division Street and Main Street, Salisbury has closed traffic and created a **pedestrian mall** (City Center) surrounded by pretty historic buildings. The area includes sophisticated women's clothing stores, several antique shops, among them **Parker Place Antiques,** and a few galleries, including the **Salisbury Art Institute and Gallery.** Also on Main, **Under the Rainbow** features a stunning collection of dolls. On Division Street, **Tyme for Tea** is a good place to stop for coffee and gaze at the Tiffany windows in Trinity Church across the street.

Several folks mentioned the **Country House** (805 E. Main St., Salisbury, 410/749-1959, www.thecountryhouse.com) as a great place to look for casual items for house and garden. The building is big—16,000 square feet—so you'll probably find more than you were looking for.

Salisbury Pewter (2611 N. Salisbury Blvd., Salisbury, 410/546-1188, www.salisburypewter .com) is the "home store" of the international company, and visitors have a chance to see the artisans at work while picking up some good buys. Pewter is a mixture of tin, copper, and antimony; during fabrication, the lead is removed, making the pewter safe for food. Those who work forming the flat pewter discs into cups and trays are called spinners—a 10-year apprenticeship is the norm—and the Salisbury Pewter trademark is applied by hand. Tiffany, the largest buyer, sells Salisbury pewter under its own trademark; the second biggest consumer of engraved pewter is the U.S. government. Check out the samples on display, and you'll see the names of several presidents.

The Centre at Salisbury, on U.S. 13 at the bypass (north of town on U.S. 13), fulfills all mall fantasies. It offers more than 90 stores and is anchored by **Boscov's, Hecht's,** and other major retailers.

An unusual shop, **Chesapeake East** (501 W. Main St., 410/546-1534) is definitely worth a stop. It's full of bright and amusing made-in-Salisbury ceramics and other local goods.

ACCOMMODATIONS

Salisbury tends to attract businesspeople, and therefore has a number of chain hotels. One of the most attractive is the **Ramada Inn** (300 S. Salisbury Blvd., 410/546-4400 or 888/800-7617, www.salisburyramada.com, $79–145). It's in a quiet south-of-downtown location and has a restaurant and indoor pool. A number of packages are available; one combines a stay with a round at local golf courses.

Another chain that offers a lot of amenities and some attractive packages is **Country Inn and Suites** (1804 Sweetbay Dr., Salisbury, 410/742-2688, www.countryinns.com,

$79–189). It features a fitness facility and indoor pool, and is southeast of downtown, not far from the University.

FOOD

Watermen's Cove (925 Snow Hill Rd., Salisbury, 410/546-1400, lunch and dinner daily, $8–26) is a cheery place and attracts a casual business lunch crowd. The menu features shrimp scampi, a seafood platter, and other seafood, chicken, and beef dishes, plus salads and sandwiches. Readers of *Metropolitan Magazine,* a Salisbury publication that serves the eastern Delmarva Peninsula, voted Watermen's Cove the best place for seafood five years in a row.

Goin' Nuts Café (947 Mt. Hermon Rd., Salisbury, 410/860-1164, lunch and dinner daily, $5–22) is a one-stop world food shop. It has a complete Italian menu, plus Thai seafood, quesadillas, bratwurst, Jamaican jerk chicken, Greek salad, Caribbean salad, broccoli tempura, and other vegetarian dishes.

Legends (City Center on Main St., Salisbury, 410/749-7717, lunch Mon.–Fri., dinner Mon.–Sat., $15–22) is an exceptional fine dining restaurant—the best in town. Charcoal-grilled filet mignon, Louisiana pasta with andouille sausage, a variety of large salads (the chicken salad has half a roasted chicken, fresh corn, and pine nuts), and the usual fresh fish dishes grace the menu. Reservations are recommended.

Greater Wicomico County

This heavily traveled area of the state has a low number of permanent residents, except in Salisbury and Ocean City. The county is rich in waterways, which made it easy for colonial farmers to get their produce to market in the big cities. The area is still green with farms, though you're just as likely to see telephone pole farms (tall, sparse pines) as golf courses these days. The importance of water travel during colonial times was emphasized by the prevalence of ferries; one that survives today is the Whitehaven Ferry, on the very southern end of the county.

RECREATION
Whitehaven Loop

This 38-mile round-trip from Salisbury is ideal for a leisurely two-day bike trip or a one-day car trip. It travels along straight two-lane roads through marshes, open fields, and "telephone-pole farms"—groves of commercially grown tall pines.

Begin on U.S. 50 in Salisbury, heading east. Make a left on Nanticoke Road, then take the first left on Pemberton Drive (south). Follow Pemberton Drive as it angles sharply right, then left. You'll pass historic **Pemberton Hall** (described in this chapter) on the left, and the **Rockawalkin Schoolhouse** near Rockawalkin Creek. Built in 1872, it's typical of one-room schoolhouses of the period. At one time, it housed 35 students in grades one through seven. It's open by appointment (call the Wicomico Historical Society, 410/860-0447).

Pemberton Drive ends at Route 349. Turn left (west) and, less than a mile, make the next left (south) on Route 352 (Whitehaven Rd.). This will take you all the way down to the **Whitehaven Ferry.**

To get some idea of how old the settlement of Whitehaven is, consider that one of the first residents was Colonel George Gale, whose first wife was George Washington's grandmother. The free ferry has been operating over the narrow stretch of the Wicomico River since 1692; it was once a link on the old colonial road between the thriving seaports of Vienna and Princess Anne. The ferry can take a car or several bicycles. It operates year-round, though hours change with the season (7 A.M.–6 P.M. Mar. 1–May 15, 6 A.M.–7:30 P.M. May 16–Sept. 15, 7 A.M.–6 P.M. Sept. 16–Oct.31, and 7 A.M.–5:30 P.M. Nov. 1–Feb. 28). It's part of the Maryland Highway System, and informa-

© JOANNE MILLER

Old Menhaden fishing boat, Whitehaven

Nutters Crossing (30287 Southampton Bridge Rd., Salisbury, 800/615-4657) is another popular semi-private club. The **Ramada Inn** offers a number of golf packages that include play at any or all of eight local courses, including those mentioned above.

ACCOMMODATIONS

If a quiet country place on the Wicomico River is your style, try the 【 **Whitehaven Hotel Historic Bed & Breakfast** (2685 Whitehaven St., Whitehaven, 410/873-2000 or 877/809-8296, www.whitehaven.tripod.com, $110–150). This Victorian beauty was built in 1810 to service travelers on the Whitehaven ferry and steamship passengers who were working their way around the Eastern Shore. Over the years, the hotel sunk deeply into a state of dilapidation; saved from the wrecking ball in 1994 by a coalition of local residents and Wicomico Historical Properties, it won the Maryland State Preservation Award in 2005. The hotel offers seven rooms with private baths.

FOOD

It's difficult not to wax rhapsodic about the 【 **Red Roost** (off Rte. 352—follow the signs, 2670 Clara Rd. Whitehaven, 410/546-5443, dinner Mar.–Oct., platters $14–19, all-you-can-eat specials $15–35). In the late 1940s, the Roost was just that—a chicken house. Chickenmeister Frank Perdue stopped by to unload feed (Perdue lived in Salisbury until his death in 2005). After a series of high tides floated away the last of the poultry in the 1960s, the place was abandoned until Frank Palmer, a car dealer from Hyattsville, attempted to turn it into a campground. The 1970s oil embargo (and the fact that the Roost was out in the middle of nowhere) kept customers away in droves. Mr. Palmer decided to experiment in the restaurant business by steaming up a few crabs and local corn. Word spread, and in 1978, when the all-you-can-eat feast was instituted, the Red Roost became an official Eastern Shore experience. Alas, the all-you-can-eat menu is restricted to fried chicken, steamed crabs, BBQ ribs, steamed shrimp, or Alaskan

tion is available at 410/548-4872. Unless you're eating or staying in the area, take the ferry across to Whitehaven Ferry Road.

Whitehaven Ferry Road dead-ends on Polks Road. Turn left (east) and continue for about five miles to Loretto-Allen Road, then turn left (north). Cross Wicomico Creek and enter the village of Allen. At the stop sign, turn right (north) and go up Allen Road, which turns into South Camden Avenue. You'll return to Salisbury on this road, passing the outlying residential areas and the pretty campus of Salisbury State University.

Golf

The Salisbury area is home to a number of golf courses, including **Elks Golf Club** (401 Church Hill Ave., Salisbury, 410/749-2695), a nine-hole, par 72 course.

Green Hill (410/749-1605, www.greenhill .com) is the local country club, in operation since 1927. This beautiful 18-hole championship golf course, ranked #2 in the state by the *Washington Times,* is open for limited public play.

snow crab legs (there are dinner platters on the menu, but why would you pass up this amazing opportunity to see just how much you can stuff down your gullet?). To loosen you up before the feast begins, the kitchen sends out platters of perfect fried chicken, corn on the cob, fried shrimp, clam strips, french fries, and homemade hushpuppies—all come with dinner. You will eat too much, guaranteed—especially if you're lubing up at the full bar. Then, if it's one of the entertainment nights (banjo, piano, Irish bands), you'll probably get up and dance and sing, too. Welcome to the Eats-tern Shore. If you can get there, go!

INFORMATION

Sandy Fulton at the **Wicomico County Convention & Visitors Bureau** (U.S. 13, Salisbury, MD, 21801, 410/548-4914 or 800/332-8687, www.wicomicotourism.org) is a real county booster and a good source of information.

Crisfield

The biggest (eight stoplights) and best-known town in Somerset County, Crisfield has long been a destination for anglers and seafood lovers. The first English settlers adopted the Native American name Annamessex for the little fishing village that was to become Somers Cove. When the railroad was extended to the harbor in 1867, the town was renamed for the man whose efforts made it all possible: John Woodland Crisfield. By 1910, the Crisfield Customs House (now a marine supplies store) boasted the largest registry of sailing vessels in the nation, and Crisfield was a boomtown. Nearby Marion may have been the strawberry capital of Maryland, but the seafood industry was always Crisfield's ace; that mainstay of 1950s Catholic Friday night dinners, Mrs. Paul's, was based in Crisfield, churning out fish stick after fish stick. Oysters were literally the foundation on which Crisfield was built: From the water tower on Eighth Street to the City Dock, the streets are laid atop billions of oyster shells. Though crabbing and commercial fishing has replaced the moribund oyster industry, Crisfield remains on top of it all.

SIGHTS
◖ Gov. J. Millard Tawes Historical Museum

The museum (Somers Cove Marina, at the end of 9th St., 410/968-2501, 9 A.M.–4:30 P.M. Mon.–Fri. and 10 A.M.–3 P.M. Sat.–Sun. Memorial Day–Oct., 9 A.M.–4:30 P.M. Mon.–Fri. Nov.–Memorial Day, $2.50) is named for a local resident and the 54th governor of Maryland. Governor Tawes was responsible for the creation of the Center for Public Broadcasting and the second span of the Chesapeake Bay Bridge, among other achievements. The museum features a well-put-together display on local marine life and its care and harvesting, as well as a section on the history of the area beginning with the native inhabitants. Rotating exhibits add interest; recently, the gallery exhibited "woolies," the embroidered renderings (usually depicting ships under full sail) of 19th-century sailors. One of the most interesting museum offerings is the **Port of Crisfield Escorted Walking Tour.** Guides take visitors through town, revealing bits of history (for instance, the fact that Charlie Adams Corner is named for an eccentric local who used to sell newspapers there) and illuminating hidden hideaways of commerce that the average visitor would miss. **Goode's Boat Yard** (GOOD-ez) has several examples of different watermen's craft in dry dock; a walk through the **Metompkin Soft Shell Crab processing plant** and **Metompkin Bay Oyster Co.** is like slipping into another era. Everything, from sorting to picking, is done by hand. Softshell crabs were the first aquaculture industry in the United States, and a mainstay of the economy here. This is an informative and fun introduction to Crisfield; the museum also offers this tour via trolley for $3.50. Another offering by the museum is the **Ward Brothers Heritage Tour,** which explores the workshop of the famous brothers who pioneered the art form of decoy carving and painting in the Jenkins Creek area. Call the museum for information on scheduled tours, and make a reservation.

In the early part of the 20th century, brothers Lem and Steve Ward, residents of Crisfield, carved some of the most sought-after duck decoys on the Chesapeake. The **Ward Brothers Workshop** (3195 Sackertown Rd.) has been restored and is open by appointment; it's part of the Crisfield Heritage Tour and may be booked through the visitors center by calling 410/968-2501.

SHOPPING

The last five blocks of Main Street leading to the City Dock in Crisfield are dotted with boutiques and gift shops. Two of note are **Jane's Accents** (907 W. Main, 410/968-0668), which carries new and consignment household items, and **This Is The Life** (529 W. Main St., 410/968-1577, www.thisisthelifeinc.net), a gift shop specializing in nautical, beach, and tropical theme items, plus work by local artists.

An out-of-town treasure, **Kings Creek Antiques & Design Center** (Rte. 13 and Perry Rd., Princess Anne, 410/651-2776, www .kingscreekantiques.com), is one of those warehouse-like multi-dealer shops that provide hours of amusement for those who love to look (and buy). You'll find lots of American/ nautical antiques and varied collectibles.

RECREATION
Cedar Island Marsh Sanctuary

Covering nearly 3,000 acres of tidal marsh, ponds, and creeks, this sanctuary in Tangier Sound near Crisfield attracts millions of black ducks in winter. In the 1960s, the black duck was declining in numbers due to loss of habitat. Today, black duck populations are on the mend, and Cedar Island is one of Maryland's best places to see the birds. Other tidal wetland wildlife species are also attracted to the area;

barn owls use nest boxes placed in the marsh to raise their young, typically between April and September. Trapping is offered by yearly lease, and crabbing, as well as fishing for sea trout, rockfish, bluefish, and spot are additional activities enjoyed by visitors. The island can only be reached by boat. The **Crisfield Heritage Foundation** (3 9th St., at the Crisfield Historical Museum, Crisfield, 410/968-2501, 9 A.M.–5 P.M. Mon.–Sat., also Sun. in summer) offers guided kayak tours for individuals, children, and families, plus photography classes. Call for a tour schedule and reservations.

Jane's Island State Park

This really beautiful public space (office 410/968-1565) on 3,100 acres includes pristine beaches, wetlands, and abundant wildlife. Eight miles of sandy beaches invite nature walks, beachcombing, picnicking, and swimming. Fifteen miles of canoe/kayak trails offer protected paddling. There are two mile-long walking trails, one with 12 exercise stations. The mainland portion of the island is accessible by car, but part of the park is accessible only by boat.

The original inhabitants, a tribe of Native Americans, left artifacts and shell mounds on the island. The latecomer Europeans used high ground for farming, and a fish processing plant operated on the south end of the island from 1877 to 1908, when menhaden fishing (an endangered species) was outlawed in Maryland. Though the plant returned and processed other fish after World War I, the stock market crash of 1929 made it unprofitable. Its 50-foot brick chimney still remains.

The park has 104 campsites, 20 of which are waterfront. Five rustic mini-cabins are available during the warmer months, and four fully equipped, full-size cabins are available year-round. The cabins all have spectacular views of the sunset, so plan to book a year in advance (888/432-2267, http://reservations.dnr .state.md.us). There are also accommodations at the island's **Daugherty Creek Conference Center** (sleeps 16—the entire center must be rented). Transient berths with hookups are available for visitors who arrive by boat. Motorboats, canoes, and kayaks may be rented at the Eagle's Nest park store. A softball field, volleyball courts, horseshoe pit, and shuffleboard area are also available.

To get to the park, take Route 358 west from Route 413. For information and reservations, call the office number listed above.

Fishing

Tangier Sound is one of the best places on the East Coast to catch fish: trout, flounder, drum, croaker, rockfish, and perch are plentiful. Aspiring anglers with their own fishing licenses may rent 16-foot fiberglass boats by the hour, half day, and full day from **Croaker Boat Rentals** (Somers Cove Marina, 410/968-3644). Crocker also offers rods and reels and ring traps for crabbing.

Head boats are a big business in Crisfield; for a complete list, contact the tourism board (410/651-2968 or 800/521-9189, www.visit somerset.com/charter_boat_captains). Visitors who choose the head boat option don't need their own licenses, as the boat captain's license covers everyone on the boat. Two speedy party boats that take visitors out for bottom fishing are **Barbara Ann II** and **Barbara Ann III** (Somers Cove Marina, Pier N, 410/957-2562). Also out of Crisfield is the **Prime Time II** (800/791-1470).

Tours

Captain Larry Laird Jr. invites visitors aboard his Chesapeake Bay workboat on the waters around Crisfield for a **Learn-It Eco-Tour** (1021 W. Main St., Crisfield, 410/968-9870). Visitors can see and hear about wildlife above the water such as ducks, geese, and osprey, and below the water: terrapins, eels, and those fast-moving, elusive oysters. Tours depart daily during the summer. Call for hours and reservations.

ACCOMMODATIONS

The **Somers Cove Motel** (700 Norris Harbor Dr., Crisfield, 888/315-2378, www.crisfield .com/somerscove, $45–85 depending on season) is a basic motel owned by the Best Value chain. Barbecue grills are available to guests, and boat launch ramps are nearby.

Bea's B&B (10 S. Somerset Ave., Crisfield, 410/968-0423, $85–100), is a nice little Victorian that's been simply restored. Three rooms either share a bath or have individual baths. Rates include breakfast.

FOOD

In the film *Star Wars,* Luke was misdirected when he was told to beware the **Dockside.** This friendly, casual restaurant (1003 W. Main St., Crisfield, 410/968-2800, breakfast, lunch, and dinner daily, $6–14) is a good place for inexpensive meals. Lots of Crisfield watermen eat here.

Also recommended: the **Side Street Seafood Restaurant** (204 S. 10th St., Crisfield, 410/968-2442, lunch and dinner daily, $7–29), which has a nice outdoor dining area; and the **Watermen's Inn,** in an old blacksmith's shop (901 W. Main, Crisfield, 410/968-2119, http://crisfield.com/watermen, 11 A.M.–9 P.M. Wed.–Fri., 8 A.M.–9:30 P.M. Sat., 8 A.M.–8 P.M. Sun. in summer, Thurs.–Sun. in winter, $6–29).

Smith Island

Accessible only by boat, Smith Island was chartered by Captain John Smith in 1608 and settled by dissenters from St. Clements Island in 1657. Many of the former Catholics converted to Methodism, which is now the only religion officially practiced here. Smith Island is made up of three bodies of land; the two southernmost are inhabited, and the northern island is the **Martin National Wildlife Refuge.**

Current denizens of Smith Island live in three small communities: Tylerton, Rhodes Point (formerly Rogue's Point, after the local pirates), and Ewell, the island's largest town. **Tylerton** is accessible by packet (mail) boat from Crisfield, and among the residences are a post office, a one-room schoolhouse, a church, and a market. **Rhodes Point** is connected to Ewell by road through the salt marsh and a wooden bridge; the only boat repair facility on Smith Island is in this tiny community. **Ewell** is the "big city," the place where the ferry boats dock and most of the island's residents can be found. The majority of the 380 Smith Islanders descended from the original colonists, cattlemen who turned to fishing by necessity. Some visitors claim that the heavy southern Maryland accent you'll hear spoken locally is reminiscent of the Elizabethan/Cornwall dialect brought here in the 18th century. The isolation of the island is highlighted by the fact that phone service wasn't available on the island until 1940, and electricity was nonexistent until 1949.

RECREATION

If you've got energy to burn, you've come to the wrong place. Smith Island will remind you that at one nearly mythical time, life wasn't lived by the clock. A walk around the streets will take about 15 minutes. A bike ride will take five minutes (you can rent bikes for $5 an hour at the booth next to the ferry dock), or you can go in style with a golf cart for $10 an hour. During your tour, you can count the multitude of shy feral cats that live off the seafood bounty.

Boat-watching is a big activity here, as is sitting. Watching people sit in their living rooms is frowned upon.

Or you can shop: **Ruke's General Store** (corner of Jones Rd. and Smith Island Rd.) is a combination flea market jumble and country store, and **Bayside Inn** (4065 Smith Island Rd.) offers souvenirs, as well as hearty meals. Both are open daily, with irregular hours (if you live there and want something, you go to the owner's house; if you came in on the boat, both shops will probably be open).

When you're done shopping, you can learn something: The **Smith Island Center** (Jones Rd. and Smith Island Rd., 410/425-3351 or 800/521-9189, www.smithisland.org/museum .html, noon–4 P.M. daily Apr.–Oct., $2) is an information and heritage museum. The center was the focus of a design award in 2003 by the American Institute of Architects.

The **Martin Wildlife Refuge** is almost

crab shack on Smith Island

© JOANNE MILLER

A VICTORY FOR TEMPERANCE?

In 1999, the Associated Press reported that a Smith Island shopkeeper's attempt to end a 300-year ban on alcohol sales on the island ended in failure. About a third of the island's 350 or so residents headed to the mainland to encourage the Somerset County liquor board to turn the liquor license down; the board voted 2-1 to deny.

The shopkeeper's request was opposed by longtime residents, many of whom are Methodists with a strong bent for temperance. The shopkeeper, who moved to Smith Island in 1997, maintained that times had changed since the island was settled in 1657, and that the sale of alcohol is a sign of progress. Some locals apparently feared the availability of alcohol would lead to fighting (those wild tourists!). The nearest police officer is a 40-minute boat ride away.

entirely salt marsh, broken up by a maze of tidal creeks and freshwater potholes. It's accessible by boat from Smith Island (the refuge is operated by the U.S. Fish and Wildlife Service, Blackwater National Wildlife Refuge, 2145 Key Wallace Dr., Cambridge, MD 21613-9536, 410/228-2692, http://northeast.fws.gov/md/mrn.htm). Visiting species change with the seasons; winter brings the heaviest populations of ducks (roughly 10,000), Canada geese (4,000), and tundra swans (1,500). Though it's possible to cruise by boat around the perimeter of the refuge, the interior is closed to the public.

ACCOMMODATIONS AND FOOD

Eating is another diversion. The **Bayside Inn** (410/425-2771) has a package deal with groups that arrive on the Tyler boats from Crisfield that includes transportation and lunch (lunch alone runs $11 for soup and a crab

sandwich to $19 for the deluxe all-you-can-eat buffet). The season starts on Memorial Day and extends to October 15—the restaurant is open 11:15 A.M.–4 P.M. during that time, and it's closed the rest of the year. If you're diabetic, pack your own food—Smith Island cuisine is heavy on nonperishable ingredients, especially sugar. It's a prominent additive to everything from stewed tomatoes to corn fritters, but you won't go away hungry. The crab soup is quite good.

There are a few places to stay in Ewell, and one in nearby Tylerton. The **Chesapeake Sunrise B&B** (Chesapeake Bay Marina, next to the Bayside Inn, Ewell, 410/425-4220, www.smithisland.us/rooms, $95–124) also offers boat slips. **Fisherman's Rest** (20930 Somers Rd. Ewell, 410/425-2095 $100) is a small cottage that's popular with visitors. The **Ewell Tide B&B** ("Turn right at the dock, we're right up the street," Ewell, 410/425-2141, $95–105) offers simple accommodations with a beautiful view. If you really want to get away from it all ("it" being roads, cars, people, and noise), take the non-vehicular ferry **Captain Jason II** from Crisfield to Tylerton (it runs at 12:30 and 5:00 P.M., $25/person round-trip, leave your car at the adjacent J.P. Tawes & Bro. Hardware parking lot in Crisfield for $3 per overnight).

Tylerton, made up of 70 residents separated by water from the rest of Smith, is the remote place you didn't think existed anymore, the community Tom Horton celebrated in his *An Island Out of Time*. Surrounded on three sides by water, **The Inn of Silent Music** (2955 Tylerton Rd., 410/425-3541, www.innofsilentmusic.com, $110–130) offers stunning views, charming rooms decorated in an eclectic style, and good food. A full breakfast is included, and you may order dinner for an additional $25. Rooms all come with bath and refrigerator. The inn closes for the season mid-November and reopens mid-March.

GETTING THERE

From Memorial Day through October, you can reach Smith Island daily via passenger cruisers captained by Otis Tyler and Terry Laird (Crisfield Dock, Crisfield, 410/968-1118 or 410/425-5931, boats leave around 12:30 P.M.), and another by Captain Alan Tyler (Tawes Museum, 410/968-2220). Reservations are necessary; round-trip fares are around $24. All year long, the smaller mail boats **Captain Jason I** and **Captain Jason II** (Crisfield, 410/425-5931) also ferry passengers to the island. The big boats cruise in style—the trip takes about an hour, and the gentle movement of the boat is very relaxing.

The mail boats are speedier and choppier; the trip takes about 35 minutes.

Mail boats and the passenger cruisers mentioned above also sail to Tangier Island, Virginia, from Crisfield. Another vessel that offers transportation is the **Steven Thomas** (City Dock, May–Oct., 410/968-2338 or 800/863-2338). Tangier Island is about the same distance from Crisfield as Smith Island and offers the same amenities, though it's slightly more developed.

Greater Somerset County

It seems the farther south you travel on the Delmarva, the more things slow down. Driving through this rich farming region, you'll pass seemingly endless fields of sorghum and soy. Local Native Americans—Pokomoke, Annamessex, Minokan, Nessawattex, and Acqintica—lived comfortably in the area, and in 1677, the largest Native American town in Maryland, Askiminokonson, existed nearby at what is now the intersection of Route 364 and U.S. 13.

Princess Anne, the county seat of Somerset County, is a sunny, one-main-street municipality, with centuries of well-preserved architecture and a well-attended house and garden tour that focuses on the town's historic past. It's also the site of the University of Maryland Eastern Shore, a modern college campus that offers a diverse curriculum. It was founded in 1886 under the auspices of the Methodist Episcopal Church and Centenary Biblical Institute of Baltimore as a school of higher learning for black Americans; today, its student body has an international profile.

In mid-May, the fish are running, and autumn is hurricane season—and they do blow through here. Deal Island and the other local destinations all offer mellow getaways and a pace reminiscent of the Deep South.

SIGHTS
Princess Anne
Founded in 1733, this town was named in honor of the 24-year-old daughter of King George II of England. Princess Anne is distinguished by many colonial-era, federal-style dwellings and mid-to-late-19th-century Victorian homes. One of these, the **Teackle Mansion** (11736 Mansion St., 410/651-2238, http://teackle.mansion.museum, 1–3 P.M. Wed., Sat., and Sun. Apr.–mid-Dec., 1–3 P.M. Sun. mid-Dec.–Mar., $6) is open for tours. Littleton and Elizabeth Teackle built the symmetrical and elegant mansion shortly after their marriage in 1800. Mr. Teackle had diverse interests as a merchant, statesman, and entrepreneur, but suffered from financial instability (possibly because of being named Little Teackle) and sold the mansion in 1839. The mansion was divided into rental properties over the years and was purchased by a local group of residents determined to preserve it in the 1950s. The Historic Princess Anne self-guided walking tour, which covers 37 other significant buildings, is available at the mansion or through the county's tourism board.

Accohannock Tribal Museum
The Accohannock (ah-co-HAH-nahk) tribe, one of the original populations on the Eastern Shore, maintains a museum in Marion, 14 miles north of Crisfield (Crisfield-Marion Rd., Marion Station). For hours of operation and more information, contact the tribe (410/623-2660, by appointment only). The museum building houses

artifacts collected and owned by the tribe, and is the site of classes in native arts and crafts. The tribe also hosts powwows and special events throughout the year, including Thanksgiving and Christmas dinners. The village (which is also the tribal home) provides easy access to Pocomoke Sound, either by canoe or pontoon boats; tours of the local bird sanctuary, wildlife refuge, and Pocomoke Sound are offered.

Deal Island

This three-mile-long spit of land is accessible by car at the end of Route 363. Ancestors of some of the current 350 inhabitants began to make a living from the sea here in 1675. **Arby's General Store** is a combination fisherman's supply store/restaurant you'll encounter when first crossing the bridge. The food is local and fresh, in spite of the sign that advertises the mouthwatering duo of bloodworms and cheese steak.

Two of the island's churches, **St. John's Methodist Episcopal** and **John Wesley United Methodist,** come complete with their own cemeteries. The epitaphs tell the story of life in a watermen's community. Graves are covered with concrete slabs; because of the high water table, they cannot be dug to the standard depth.

The island's 20-vessel skipjack contingent—the last of the 19th-century oyster fleet—is docked at the end of the road, in the village of **Wenona.** To see them, it's best to come late in the day, when they return from harvesting on the bay. There's a skipjack race every Labor Day weekend. Get the latest Deal Island news at www.dealislandmaryland.com.

ACCOMMODATIONS

◖**Waterloo Country Inn** (28822 Mt. Vernon Rd., Princess Anne, 410/651-0883, $125–255 Apr. 1–Oct. 31, $125–225 off-season) is the place to go for a romantic getaway in elegant surroundings. Henry Waggaman, a wealthy local landowner, built the house in 1750 as a showplace residence. Like many properties that lie some distance from an urban center, the manor suffered years of neglect before being lovingly restored by Theresa and Erwin Kraemer, who emigrated from Switzerland in 1995.

They came upon the crumbling edifice while visiting friends in the area, fell in love with it, and took the necessary actions to refurbish it and turn it into a wonderful B&B. Rooms are tastefully decorated in the Victorian style.

Canoes are available for guest use, and the nearby waterways are a haven for migrating Canada geese and other waterfowl. Paddling along during the late afternoon is an almost surreal experience. The inn also has a swimming pool and bicycles for guests.

The Waterloo serves dinner by advance request—the menu is a sophisticated blend of American and Swiss entrées—and occasionally hosts special events. If you'd prefer peace and quiet, make sure your visit doesn't coincide with one of these. Breakfast is included with an overnight stay.

FOOD

Peaky's (30361 Mt. Vernon Rd., Princess Anne, 410/651-1950, lunch and dinner daily, lunch $7, dinner $14) is owned, as you might expect, by the Peacocks—Greg and Anne. It's the hot spot in the area; everybody seems to eat here all at once. The good news is there's plenty of room. The menu is classic American diner: grilled ham-and-cheese sandwiches, fried chicken, rack of pork ribs. The prices are classic, too, and the pies are homemade.

If you're looking for a quick, inexpensive sandwich or supplies for several days, go to **Lankford Sysco Food Services** at the intersection of Route 667 and U.S. 13. The company store there has a deli and a grocery/produce store. You may not need a 20-pound bag of ginger snaps, but even small items are priced reasonably.

Allegro Coffee & Tea Salon (11775 Somerset Ave., 6A, Princess Anne, 410/651-4520) is a homey stop for a quick cup and a leisurely browse among the gift items for sale.

SOMERSET COUNTY INFORMATION

Contact **Somerset County Tourism** (P.O. Box 243, Princess Anne, MD 21853, 410/651-2968 or 800/521-9189, www.visitsomerset.com).

Snow Hill

Snow Hill, the county seat of Worcester, was settled in 1642 and made its mark as a trading port for schooners and steamboats. Today, the sedate river town offers a quiet getaway with stately B&Bs, a fine small museum, a historic village built around a peat-fired furnace, and canoe trips on the mirror-like Pocomoke River.

SIGHTS
Julia A. Purnell Museum

This museum (208 W. Market St., 410/632-0515, www.purnellmuseum.com, 10 A.M.–4 P.M. Tues.–Sat. and 1–4 P.M. Sun. Apr.–Oct., adults $2) is named in honor of the mother of a local resident. At the age of 85, a fall confined Mrs. Purnell to a wheelchair; she took up folk art needlework and completed more than 1,000 pictures before her death in 1943—two months after her 100th birthday, and two years after she was inducted into the National Hobby Hall of Fame. Many of her pictures depict historic buildings and scenes from Snow Hill, and the museum continues to focus on local history. Tools, toys, machines, curios, and clothing are exhibited, along with their stories. Though many small museums fall into the dusty-cabinet category, this one makes the displays lively and colorful. In keeping with Mrs. Purnell's love of needlework, the museum holds the Delmarva Needle Art Show and Competition in September. If you're expecting grandma's embroidered linens, you're in for a surprise. Submissions include cross-stitch, embroidery, tatting, lace, quilting, and appliqué, all expertly done—and some so fantastically modern that the old techniques seem new again. One recent award winner was a portrait done in sepia-toned yarns that was indistinguishable from a photograph. This has to be seen to be appreciated.

Historic Homes of Snow Hill

While walking around the historic homes of Snow Hill (a walking tour brochure is available at the Purnell museum or from Worcester County Tourism), you might come across the **Mt. Zion One-Room School Museum** (Church and Ironshire Sts., www.octhebeach.com/museum/zion.html, $2), which was moved to Snow Hill from the countryside and opened to the public in 1964. The school contains 19th-century texts and furnishings. It's open 1–4 P.M. Tuesday–Saturday mid-June–September 7. One of the loveliest of the area's public historic homes is **Costen House** (206 Market St., 410/957-3110, 1–4 P.M. Wed.–Sat. May–Oct., $2), a Queen Anne Victorian with extensive gardens that once was home to the mayor of Pocomoke.

Furnace Town

This restored village (Old Furnace Rd., four miles north of Snow Hill 410/632-2032, www.furnacetown.com, 10 A.M.–5 P.M. daily Apr.–Oct., $4 adults) is built around an iron furnace once fueled by bog-ore; in the 1840s, the furnace was a feat of mechanical engineering unmatched in the state. During its nearly 80 years of operation, it was converted from the standard cold-blast method to the high-tech (for the 19th century) hot-blast method using an innovative system of recirculated heated air. Various artisans demonstrate 19th-century crafts in the village buildings and on the grounds.

The village includes a museum, woodworker's cottage, weaver's house, blacksmith shop, print shop, woodworkers shop, and the Old Nazareth Church. Off the main parking lot, the Nature Conservancy maintains an easy mile-long trail through the Pocomoke Forest and over the **Nassawango Cypress Swamp**. The preserve is open year-round, and Nassawango Creek is banked by centuries-old bald cypress and black gum trees. One way to appreciate the serene beauty of the area is by canoe, between Nassawango Road and Red House Road. This is a two-mile route, and canoes may be launched on Red House Road, or it can be reached from Snow Hill via the Pocomoke River—about three miles away. Canoes may be rented in Snow Hill.

To get to Furnace Town by car from Snow Hill, take Route 12 north five miles. Turn left (west) on Old Furnace Road, and proceed for one mile. Furnace Town is on the left. Furnace Town often holds special events, such as a 19th-century Christmas church service in December and the Worcester County Fair in August.

RECREATION

The Pocomoke is an exceptionally beautiful and uncrowded black-water river. The most fun way to see it is by canoe or kayak. The **Pocomoke River Canoe Co.** (312 N. Washington St., 410/632-3971 or 800/258-0905) rents both (and 14-foot aluminum boats) by the hour, day, or weekend. It also offers trips that include portage to the put-in and take-out sites.

ACCOMMODATIONS

The **River House Inn** (201 E. Market, Snow Hill, 410/632-2722, www.riverhouseinn.com) offers two deluxe cottages and two apartments

© JOANNE MILLER

Furnace Town steam vents

in a separate building set on more than two acres of rolling lawns that lead down to the Pocomoke River. The Riverview Hideaways features two suites, both with mini-fridges and microwaves ($250 each); the River Cottage ($250) carriage barn has a microwave, fridge, and coffeemaker; the Ivy Cottage ($300) features all the comforts of home: fireplace, hot tub, TV, dining area, 1.5 baths, a full kitchen, and a bedroom upstairs. Larry and Susanne Knudsen have restored the house and outbuildings to their former Greek Revival glory, and they furnished everything in period style. The covered porches provide space for luxurious naps on hot summer afternoons, and the Adirondack chairs on the river's edge have armrests big enough for a wineglass.

The Mansion House Bed & Breakfast (4436 Bayside Rd., Public Landing, Snow Hill, 410/632-3189, www.mansionhousebnb.com, rooms $140–160, Sunset Cottage $150–300 per night or $1,000 per week) is on the National Register of Historic Places. The property overlooks a broad expanse of Chincoteague Bay with Assateague Island in the distance. This planter's residence was built around 1835 and has been carefully restored to its original charm, It's located in the village of Public Landing, about five miles from Snow Hill. The four guest rooms in the Mansion House all have private baths, fireplaces, and three feature a water view. Sunset cottage is two blocks from the main house, and has a view of Paw Paw Creek and the Chincoteague Bay.

FOOD

A few local recommendations are: **Palette** (104 W. Green St., 410/632-0055, dinner Tues.–Sat. $12–25) for fare with a French twist; **Take 2 Scoops** (111 Pearl St., 410/632-3933) for great homemade ice cream; **China Moon** (305 E. Market St., 410/632-0885, lunch and dinner daily, $6–17) for American Chinese; **Tavern on Green Street** (208 West Green St., 410/632-5451, lunch and dinner daily, $5–18) for pub food; and **My Sister's Place** (5610 B Market St., 410/632-1154, breakfast and lunch Mon.–Sat., $6–20) for sandwiches and light meals.

Berlin

Colonial travelers once looked forward to this stop on the old Philadelphia Post Road, mainly due to the Burleigh Inn. In fact, the village name is thought to be a contraction of Burleigh Inn, hence the emphasis on the first syllable (BUR-lin, as in "I was burlin' through town when I saw the police car"). The inn is no more, but this pretty little town has a wonderful hotel and a number of historic homes among its tree-lined streets. If you saw the film *Runaway Bride,* with Richard Gere and Julia Roberts, you got an eyeful of Berlin. Besides being Hollywood's version of a small midwestern town, it's a popular place to stop on the way to or from Ocean City.

SIGHTS
Calvin B. Taylor House Museum

One of Berlin's historic homes is open to the public (Main and Baker Sts., 410/641-1019, www.taylorhousemuseum.org). The Taylor House gives visitors an inside look at 19th-century decorative arts and features a collection of local memorabilia. It's open 1–4 P.M. Monday, Wednesday, Friday, and Saturday from Memorial Day to October. Donations are appreciated.

ACCOMMODATIONS

The **Atlantic Hotel** (2 N. Main St., 410/641-3589 or 800/814-7672, www.atlantichotel.com, standard $85–180, deluxe $115–215) is so modern and meticulous, you wouldn't know that it's been around since 1895. But much of that Victorian flavor is retained—the rooms are spacious, with all the amenities, and the hotel has an elevator, a rarity in vintage buildings. This is a pleasant, well-run hotel that also offers an apartment and cottage ($140–230). Room rates depend on season and day of the week; midweek winter rates are always lowest. Richard Gere himself slept at the Atlantic and

© JOANNE MILLER

Atlantic Hotel

the hotel staff found him "real nice and down-to-earth" and "good-looking in person, but shorter than I thought."

Merry Sherwood Plantation (8909 Worcester Hwy., Berlin, 410/641-2112 or 800/660-0358, www.merrysherwood.com, $100–175 mid-Oct.–mid-May, $125–200 mid-May–mid-Oct.) was built in 1859, the result of a union between a wealthy Philadelphian, Henry Johnson, and a local girl, Elizabeth Henry. There are five rooms with private baths, two rooms with a shared bath, and a honeymoon suite. Ms. Henry's father requested that a suitable house be built for his daughter on the property given as her dowry. The 8,500-square-foot Italianate/Greek Revival structure was designed for lavish parties, with enough bedrooms to put guests up for long periods of time. It's fitting, then, that it's become an elegant country inn. The building and grounds are popular for weddings and receptions, so call ahead to see if a room is available.

FOOD

The Atlantic hotel (2 N. Main St., 410/641-3589 or 800/814-7672, www.atlantic hotel.com) has an excellent restaurant, **◖ Solstice,** with dinner entrées like butter-poached beef ribeye with roast potatoes and chimichurri brown butter ($26) and pan roast wild rockfish with roasted carrots, cauliflower, and salsify in a red-wine bacon sauce ($25). Solstice serves a less formal menu for lunch, including pork and beans (smoky black bean soup with a spicy pork and butternut squash salad, $10) and a grilled angus chuck burger with smoked bacon, blue cheese pickled red onion and rocket greens on ciabatta ($10).

The **Globe Theater and Café** (12 Broad St., Berlin, 410/641-0784, www.globetheater.com), serves breakfast, lunch, and dinner daily in addition to hosting art displays and music events. Soups and sandwiches range $5–12, and dinner entrées range $19–28. It's open daily, and there are lots of specials. Brunch on Sunday is often accompanied by live music.

Ocean City

The biggest destination in Worcester County and Maryland's Eastern Shore is Ocean City, "Miami of the North"—so nicknamed because of the 10-mile strip of fancy resort hotels and condos that line the beach and bay. Yet it's not nearly as tacky as its southern namesake or even nearby Atlantic City, saved by a lack of casinos, limited development space, and an emphasis on the beach. And what a beach it is. A seemingly endless swath of soft beige sand extends along most of the peninsula, and the wide boardwalk itself is several miles long. In the summer, brightly colored umbrellas (for rent on the beach) provide shade and color in the white-hot sun, and at night, the boardwalk is merry with strolling couples, singles, and families. Getting around is easy; there are two main north–south streets (Philadelphia heading south and Baltimore heading north—both turn into Coastal Highway above 33rd St.). Addresses are sometimes indicated as "oceanside" (closer to the Atlantic), "oceanfront" (on the beach), or "bayside" (closer to Isle of Wight Bay).

For a spot with so many part-time residents and visitors, you'd expect everything from wax museums to shell collections—not here. A few attractions aimed at tourists have been around for a while and have somehow managed to escape the oily, worn funkiness of such places. Newer attractions are squeaky clean. The city refers to itself as "The East Coast's Number One Family Resort," and it's easy to see why.

There's enough to do in town to satisfy every taste and time limit. You could spend two weeks on the miniature golf courses alone, and several standard-size courses are within easy driving distance. The beaches of southern Delaware are all within an hour by auto. Atlantic fishing is a major pastime, as is horse racing. And Ocean City has its quirks: Along the boardwalk, there's an artist who makes sand sculptures by moonlight; his creations are there to greet beachgoers the next day. Incredibly detailed, the sculptures all have religious themes, often illustrating a quote from the Bible.

If you need refueling after all the sights and activities, Ocean City is famous for its "beach food": the ultimate munchie triumvirate of Thrasher's french fries, Dumser's ice cream, and Fisher's caramel corn. There are cheap places to eat and expensive places to eat, classic and avant-garde menus. You won't be bored, guaranteed.

SIGHTS
◖ Ocean City Boardwalk

Stretching from the inlet north past 27th Street, the boardwalk functions as a chronological history of this fishing village/resort. During the day, trams run the full length of the boardwalk; tickets are $2.75–3 and include frequent stops. The oldest and most active part of the boardwalk is between the inlet on South First Street and Eighth Street. The inlet itself didn't exist until a 1933 storm removed a swath of land that connected Assateague Island with Ocean City. Locals liked the new bay access so much, they continued to dredge the inlet to keep it open.

In 1976, sculptor Peter Toth placed his 21st carving at the base of the inlet. The artist had vowed to create works that would honor Native Americans, one for each state. He dedicated the 30-foot-tall, 100-year-old oak carving to the local Choptanks, Nacotchtanks, Chapticons, and Nanticokes. The sculpture, dubbed the *Inlet Indian*, serves as his memorial to the first people.

At the beginning of the boardwalk, just beyond the inlet Indian, the Ocean City Life-Saving Station Museum sits on the location of a U.S. Coast Guard lifesaving station designated by the federal government in 1878. Surfmen patrolled the beach on foot and horseback, watching for foundering vessels. The station was in use until 1964, when a new station was built on the bayside.

A little farther north, Trimper's Rides began in 1902 with the installation of a steam-powered 45-animal carousel, and has been expanded since.

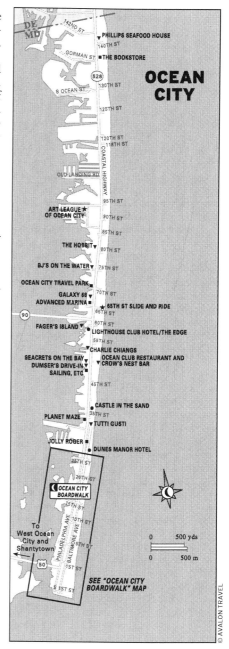

Grandparents now bring their grandchildren to ride their favorite steeds or sit on the carousel's rocking chair.

Taylor's Ocean Pier was completed in 1907, offering visitors a place for line fishing and trapshooting. Destroyed by fire in 1925, the city built a larger pier, complete with a frame building used as a convention hall and teen center. The building has been remodeled to hold souvenir shops and concessions.

In 1905, Rudolph Dolle, a candy-maker from New York, began his business on the boardwalk. He lived over the store and hand-pulled his most famous creation: salt-water taffy. **Dolle's Candyland** has been owned and operated by generations of the same family.

Women played a major role in the development of Ocean City as a resort destination. Lizzie Hearne turned her eight-room beach house off Dorchester Street into a hotel in 1905. A nearby cottage, the Belmont, was joined to the Hearne property, and the **Belmont-Hearn Hotel** is currently run by the fourth and fifth generations of the original family. The **Lankford Hotel** is another example. Several hotels still in operation a block from the boardwalk were also built around this time: Josephine Hastings converted her house and two adjacent cottages into the **Avelon Inn** (1st and N. Baltimore Sts.—note that S. 1st St. is on the inlet, and 1st St. is several blocks north). Ms. Hastings also built the **Atlantic House** (N. Baltimore between 5th and 6th Streets).

Two blocks west of the boardwalk, at 502 South Philadelphia Avenue, **Dumser's** has built a replica of its original pier building that stood on the boardwalk. Inside, a full-scale manufacturing plant is on view, and visitors can enjoy a sundae in the adjacent ice cream parlor.

The remainder of the boardwalk contains the usual compendium of souvenir shops and T-shirt emporiums, and a smattering of restaurants and fast-food places. Their doors blow open with the late spring winds and slam shut with the arrival of autumn. But Ocean City will continue on, with the boardwalk as its backbone.

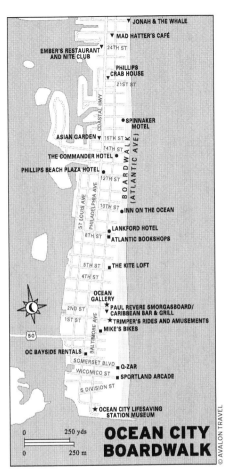

OCEAN CITY BOARDWALK

© AVALON TRAVEL

Amusement Parks

Probably the oldest ongoing attraction in Ocean City is **Trimper's Rides and Amusements** (Baltimore and 1st Sts. on the boardwalk and fishing pier, www.beach-net.com/trimpers), which has been around since the early 1900s. But the whirling rides, brightly lit games, and mechanical fortune-tellers are so well maintained that the only real reference to Coney Island is an antique Coney Island–style Herschel-Spellman merry-go-round, glittering with jewels and fantasy animals.

© JOANNE MILLER

Ocean City's finest

Daniel Trimper bought the massive carousel in 1902—the only other carousel similar to this one, incidentally at Coney Island, was destroyed by fire. There's plenty of neon, skill games, Ferris wheels, merry-go-rounds, and bumper rides—more than 100 in all—so kids won't be at all disappointed. It's open year-round—during the warm months, the hours are noon–midnight on weekends, 1 P.M.–midnight during the week. As the weather cools down, the hours become shorter and some rides shut down. Tickets may be purchased in blocks or by single ride.

Jolly Roger (30th St. and Coastal Hwy., 410/289-3477, www.jollyrogerpark.com, 9 A.M.–5 P.M. Apr.–Memorial Day, 9 A.M.–midnight Memorial Day–Labor Day, 9 A.M.–6 P.M. Labor Day–Oct. 9 and Oct. weekends, closed Nov.–Mar., not all amusements open at all hours) is the city's largest family entertainment center, with a water park, car racing, miniature golf, rides, games, and concessions. Rates are based on individual amusements.

One of the newer mini-amusement parks in town is **65th St. Slide & Ride** (bayside at 65th St., 410/524-5270, www.slidenride.com, 10 A.M.–6 P.M. May–June and Sept., later hours July–Aug., closed Oct.–Apr.), with water slides, miniature golf, batting cages, bumper boats, and more.

Planet Maze (33rd Street and Coastal Highway, 410/524-4386, wwwlplanetmaze.com) is open year-round, offering water play such as indoor and outdoor tubes and slides, tunnels, and a misty maze for hot days. There's a video arcade for the less active. It's open weekdays 10 A.M.–6 P.M. (until 9 P.M. weekends) and stays open until midnight Memorial Day–Labor Day. Winter hours vary, so call or visit the website to confirm.

There are two laser-tag places in town, both with high-tech arcades. **Laser Storm** (33rd St. and Coastal Hwy., part of Planet Maze) offers a "Stargate" arena. **Q-Zar** (401 S. Atlantic Ave./boardwalk, 410/289-2266, www.oceancity.com/q-zar, 9 A.M.–2 A.M.) is right off the beach. Both are open year-round.

Frontier Town Western Theme Park (Rte.

KRAZY GOLF

Ocean City is Fantasy Island when it comes to miniature golf. Local course owners try to outdo each other with themes, exemplified by figures and settings made of chicken wire and plaster, enhanced by imagination and a creative sense of geography. Ice Land Golf, at the south end of the peninsula, is notable for oversized polar bears and frolicking penguins; Hawaiian Gardens relies on the tiki torch, as does the Polynesian section of the 136th Street triple course. The other two courses on the property are Pirate (masted ships, peg legs, and parrots) and Safari (elephants, lions, and giraffes). Viewed from the street, this one presents a very confused cultural picture.

While our imaginations are primed, it would be a fantasy violation to leave out Medieval Castle & Big Top Circus, and Dinosaurs! & Indoor Underwater. Somewhere, people are making big bucks creating giant clown heads and life-size rubber pterodactyls. Meanwhile, right here in Ocean City, visitors can spend many a lazy evening swinging miniature putters over a gargling sea monster, or aiming between the legs of a dancing suit of armor. If all else fails, return to the Garden of Eden. You can go home again.

- **Bamboo Golf:** 3rd Street and Philadelphia, 410/289-3374

- **Doughroller Bamboo Golf:** 41st Street and Philadelphia, 410/524-2476

- **Garden of Eden:** 19th Street and Philadelphia, 410/289-5495

- **Ice Land Golf:** 400 South Philadelphia Street, 410/289-0443

- **Jungle Golf:** 30th Street and Philadelphia, 410/289-4902

- **Maui Golf:** 57th Street and Philadelphia, 410/424-8804

- **Old Pro Golf Dinosaurs! & Indoor Underwater:** 68th Street, 410/524-2645

- **Old Pro Golf Lost Temple:** 23rd Street and Coastal Highway, 410/289-6501

- **Old Pro Golf Medieval Faire:** 28th Street, 410/289-9286

- **Old Pro Golf Pirate, Safari, & Polynesian:** 136th Street, 410/524-2645

And on the Delaware border above 145th Street:

- **Fen-Tiki Golf:** Fenwick Avenue and Coastal Highway, 302/537-9779

- **Golf Down Under:** Route 54 and Coastal Highway, 302/539-1199

611, West Ocean City, 410/641-0057, www .frontiertown.com, 10 A.M.–6 P.M. mid-June–Labor Day) has developed the Disney concept of Frontierland into an entire park. Wild West shows, gunfights, paddle boats, trail rides, Indian dancing—one admission covers it all.

Baja Amusements (12639 Ocean Gateway/ U.S. 50, West Ocean City, 410/213-2252, www.bajaoc.com) offers a large go-kart track, just west of the city. It's open 9 A.M.–midnight during the warm months, and 9 A.M.–sunset October 1–November 15.

Sportland Arcade (506 S. Atlantic Ave./ boardwalk at Wicomico Street, 410/289-4987) offers the latest electronic games, along with virtual reality theater. Up to 20 people can participate together, competing with each other to play out scenes. There's also a section of "Las Vegas–style" games with the opportunity to win tickets that can be converted to prizes. Call for hours.

Art Galleries
Ocean Gallery (2nd St. at the boardwalk, 410/289-5300, www.oceangallery.com) isn't really an art gallery, unless you're seriously looking for paint-by-numbers seascapes, those big rolling ocean pictures of the sort that decorate motels located several hundred miles from saltwater. The real art here is the building it-

self, which is made of nailed and pasted-together bits of wood, parts of torn paintings, signs, and other flotsam. Once in a while, an equally flamboyant art car encrusted with leftovers from the building's exterior is parked on the street outside.

The **Art League of Ocean City** (516 94th St., 410/524-9433, www.artleagueofoceancity .org, 11 A.M.–4 P.M. Tues.–Thurs. and 1–4 P.M. Fri.–Sun. year-round, free) is a community-oriented organization that sponsors classes, workshops, and a public art exhibit (no paint-by-numbers here). Meet the artists at a reception held the first Friday of each month (5–7 P.M.).

Museums

Ocean City Life-Saving Station Museum

(boardwalk at the inlet, 410/289-4991, www .ocmuseum.org, 10 A.M.–10 P.M. daily June–Sept., 10 A.M.–4 P.M. daily May and Oct., $3) is a fascinating small museum that preserves the history of the U.S. Life-Saving Service, telling the story of the heroes who were always at the ready to rescue passengers and crew from downed ships. Call for winter hours. The museum also focuses on Ocean City and its past. Exhibits change regularly; a recent one displayed delightfully kitschy shell-covered souvenirs from the town's past—jewel boxes and mermaids, mirrors and salt shakers. The museum's displays are both informative and charming; who could resist a collection of sand from around the world and dollhouse-sized models of local hotels and businesses? It's a fond look at a resort that's been functioning for more than a century. Don't let the big shark get you!

Wheels of Yesterday (12708 Ocean Gateway, West Ocean City, 410/213-7329, www .wheelsofyesterday.com, 9 A.M.–9 P.M. June–Sept., 9 A.M.–5 P.M. Oct.–May, $4) is a must-see for car buffs, especially those with an eye for classic models. The 1928 Lincoln Overland touring car used in Jack Benny's TV program during the 1950s is here, as is an 1830 rural mail delivery wagon and a 1934 racing car, all in prime condition. There's an early version of a recreational vehicle, and an intact 1950s service station.

ENTERTAINMENT
Nightlife

Ocean City has a major bar scene at night, sometimes featuring live music. The acknowledged premier spot in town, which many other night spots are modeled after, is **Seacrets** (49th St. and bayside, 410/524-4900, www .seacrets.com, lunch and dinner daily). It serves food and drinks on a year-round artificial beach that is so Jamaican in execution, you'd be hard-pressed to remember you're in Maryland after a couple of rum drinks. The owner was the first to bring in palm trees and keep them alive by heroic measures during the intemperate winters. Seacrets is definitely still the hippest place in town, and it features live entertainment nearly every night. Get ready to shuffle to reggae—don't worry, be irie, but don't call the bartender "Ay, mon."

The **Caribbean Bar & Grill** (2nd and boardwalk in the Plim Plaza Hotel, 410/289-6181) is definitely an imitation, but has the advantage of being on the boards and next to Revere's Smorgasbord, so you can either enjoy the Caribbean's pub menu or stagger off next door to ingest large quantities of food. Live entertainment on the weekends.

Fager's Island (60th on the bay, 410/524-5400, www.fagers.com, lunch and dinner daily) is also a popular restaurant, with Pacific Rim cuisine, half-price specials, and Sunday brunch. It's open year-round and has a variety of live entertainment (soul, rock, Top 40) and late-night action every night. Fager's has nine brews on draft and a tequila bar. Try to make it for the sunset; the restaurant pipes in Tchaikovsky's *1812 Overture* as the bay turns bright orange.

The **Ocean Club Restaurant & Crow's Nest Bar** (49th St. at the beach, 800/638-2100, www.clarionoc.com/nightlife, lunch and dinner daily) has a great view of the beach, but it's the live entertainment and dancing most nights that brings 'em in. The restaurant is all wood and arched windows, with a view of the "tropical" beach, and the open-air bar is on the second floor. Both facilities are attached to a resort hotel, the Clarion.

BJ's on the Water (75th St. at the bay,

410/524-7575, www.bjsonthewater.com) is another restaurant that offers entertainment nearly every night; bands range from blues to zydeco, hard rock to jazz.

SHOPPING
Antiques and Collectibles

The **Seaport Antique Village** (six miles west of Ocean City on Rte. 54, 302/436-8962) is actually in tax-free Delaware; it features 25 dealers and a variety of merchandise and is open daily year-round. **Ocean Downs Flea Market** (at Bally's racetrack, U.S. 50 and Rte. 589) takes place every weekend in September.

Malls

Shantytown, just west of the bridge on U.S. 50 in West Ocean City, is where the fishing boats depart from. It's an interesting little village made up of individual shops. Of course, Ocean City has a big **Factory Outlet** mall, with Bass, Ann Taylor, Haggar, Reebok, and so on. It's at U.S. 50 and Golf Course Road, 0.5 mile west of the U.S. 50 bridge in West Ocean City.

Books

The **Mason Collection** in Shantytown Village is a book lover's paradise, with thousands of used books for sale. **The Bookstore** (137th St. and Coastal Hwy.) specializes in mysteries, but features all sorts of new and used books. **Atlantic Bookshops** (701 N. Atlantic Ave., 410/289-1776) is the place to go for new and shiny volumes. It also has outlets in Rehoboth Beach and Bethany Beach, Delaware.

Specialty Shops

One of the most popular shops in Ocean City is **The Kite Loft** (5th St. at boardwalk, 410/289-7855, and 131st St. and Coastal Hwy., 410/250-4970, www.kiteloft.com). As you might expect, kites are a big pastime on the beach, and this shop has a wide variety.

RECREATION
Bicycles

Mikes Bikes (N. Division St. and Baltimore Ave., 410/289-5404) rents bikes year-round.

On the Water

Sailing, Etc. (46th St. at the bay, 410/723-1144) rents inline skates, windsurfers, parasails, sailboats, and kayaks and includes lessons on the use of each.

O.C. Bayside Rentals (Dorchester St. at the Olde Town Marina, 410/289-7112) is the place for jet boats and pontoon boats.

Advanced Marina (66th St. at the bay, 410/723-2124) is a complete marine store with fishing equipment and waverunners, water skis, and ski tubes for rent.

The **O.C. Fishing Center** (Rte. 50, West Ocean City, 800/322-3065, www.ocfishing.com) lists a number of charter boats available for anglers of all skill levels.

The **O.C. Rocket** (Talbot St. pier, 410/289-3500, www.talbotstreetpier.com/boat rides), a speedboat, conducts dolphin-, bird-, and whale-watching expeditions that sometimes include a cruise by Assateague Island to spot wild ponies.

NOT-SO-KRAZY GOLF

Worcester County has dozens of challenging courses, including:

- **Deer Run:** 8804 Logtown Road, Berlin, 410/629-0060 or 800/790-4465, www.golfdeerrun.com.

- **Nutters Crossing:** 30287 Southampton Bridge Road, Salisbury, 410/860-4653 or 800/615-4657, www.nutterscrossing.com

- **Ocean City Golf Club:** 11401 Country Club Drive, Berlin, 410/641-1779 or 800/442-3570, www.oceancitygolfclub.com

- **River Run:** Beauchamp Road off Route 589, Ocean City, 410/641-7200 or 800/733-7786, www.riverrungolf.com (designed by Gary Player).

- **Rum Pointe:** 7000 Rum Pointe Lane, Berlin, 410/629-1414 or 888/809-4653.

Golf

Here are a few of many choices, all open year-round: **Rum Pointe Seaside Golf Links** (700 Rum Pointe Ln., Berlin, 410/629-1414 or 888/809-4653, www.rumpointe.com); **Ocean City Golf Club** (11401 Country Club Dr., Berlin, 410/641-1779 or 800/422-3570, www.oceancitygolfclub); and **Eagle's Landing** (12367 Eagle's Nest Rd., West Ocean City, 410/213-7277 or 800/283-3846, www.eagles landinggolf.com).

Harness Racing

At **Ocean Downs** (Rtes. 50 and 589, officially in Berlin, but less than one mile west of Ocean City, 410/641-0600, www.oceandowns.com), the ponies race with tiny carts behind them during the summer months. Simulcast racing is available year-round if you just need to see horses run really fast. The track restaurant offers specials on Friday and Sunday.

ACCOMMODATIONS

Lodging in Ocean City can be broken down into five subsections: big hotels, small hotels, B&Bs and inns, condo rentals, camping, and, for the truly budget-minded, sleeping in doorways. The last is recommended for those traveling close to the bone, as it's difficult to get a roof over the old noggin for less than $130 a night in season (weekdays in winter are a different story). Rates run roughly $60 per night in the low season, up to $300 in the high season, regardless of the lodging you choose. Weekly stays are discounted.

To complicate matters, each lodging's "season"—and the higher prices associated with it—is slightly different. Many accommodations are on the boardwalk—the advantage being instant access to the beach, the disadvantages (below 8th St.) being crowds and noise, more during the day than at night. Quite a few apartments are on the main streets—Baltimore heading north and Philadelphia heading south, and the cross-streets. Prices are better, but traffic is heavy all the way up the peninsula during the day, somewhat less at night. The cross-streets are slightly better, but since the blocks are so

narrow, the improvement is slight. Your best bet for a quiet night is the boardwalk above 8th Street or cross streets right off the boardwalk. The following listings represent what's available. Whatever accommodation you choose, you're never more than a short stroll to the beach.

Big Hotels

Many hotels have been in operation for decades, and like all big hotels, some portion is usually being renovated. These are the rooms to ask for; the older rooms are sometimes comically small, with mattresses that offer support equivalent to stale marshmallows.

The Commander Hotel (oceanfront at 14th and the boardwalk, Ocean City, 410/289-6166 or 888/289-6166, www.commanderhotel.com, mid-Mar.–mid-Nov.) was called the "Grand Lady" and "Jewel of the Boardwalk" when it was built in 1930 by Mrs. Minnie Lynch. Innovations included an elevator and a telephone switchboard. It's now owned by fourth-generation members of the Lynch family, and has been completely modernized over the years. For an indirect oceanview efficiency on the side of the building, rates range from a rock-bottom March–April $65 weekday to $209 for a weekend night. For an oceanfront view suite, rates for those time periods are $82–279. Weekly rates are slightly lower. Lowest rates are for efficiencies with one double bed and a small refrigerator. Higher rates reflect oceanfront views, large suites with a refrigerator and a microwave, two double beds, and a private balcony. Cabanas have private balconies, full-size refrigerators, two double beds, and microwaves; they're located in the back section of the building away from the ocean and run $69–252 per night, depending on the season. The Commander also rents two-bedroom apartments by the week that range $795–1,795, depending on the season. Parking is free (a major advantage), and the hotel features indoor and outdoor pools and a guest laundry. It also offers golf packages.

Phillips Beach Plaza Hotel (1301 Atlantic Ave./boardwalk, 410/289-9121 or 800/492-5834, www.phillipsbeachplaza.com, Mar.–Dec.) has its front entrance on a side street but is actually on the beach, near 13th Street. This is the place to indulge your Victorian fantasies, right down to the heavy ruby-colored velvet draperies and crystal chandeliers. The hotel features a cozy bar and fancy restaurant (below). Rooms range $45–170 per day (no ocean view or limited ocean view) and $55–185 (ocean view), depending on the season (high season is June 25–Aug. 22). The hotel also offers lodgings ranging from small efficiencies to three-bedroom apartments, all with full kitchens, from $65–275 per day, seasonally adjusted. Weekly rates are lower. Golf packages and three-day/two-night specials with breakfast and dinner are available.

The **Dunes Manor Hotel** (28th St., one block from the boardwalk, 410/289-1100 or 800/523-2888, www.dunesmanor.com, year-round) is a modern take on the Victorian theme—think Victoria in the tropics without half her luggage. The hotel was built in 1987 and features an indoor-outdoor pool, a fitness room, and a restaurant and lounge. Word has gotten out about the free afternoon tea 3–4 P.M., so the number of "guests" in the hotel seems to double during that hour. Parking is free for one car per room. All rooms have an oceanfront view and private balcony, and rates run $45–289 per day. High season is June 28–September 1. Two types of efficiency apartments are offered, with rates ranging $109–355 per day. Packages are available.

Castle in the Sand (oceanfront at 37th St., 410/289-6846 or 800/522-7263, www.castle inthesand.com, Feb.–Nov.) is close to the Ocean City Convention Center and boasts a wide array of lodgings, from standard hotel rooms to two-bedroom cottage apartments. A 25-meter Olympic-size pool is nestled among the hotel's buildings. Some rooms feature a glass wall to take in the ocean view, others have balconies. Not all rooms have an ocean view. Rates range $69–239 per day, $395–1,895 per week for rooms and suites. Efficiency apartments range $79–279 per day, $465–1,475 per week. The high season is roughly mid-June–late August. The Castle offers good packages, plus substantial discounts for seniors.

Small Hotels, B&Bs, and Inns

Keep in mind that the older, less expensive boardwalk hotels and basic motels are often booked far in advance by regulars who come back every year.

The **Lankford Hotel** (boardwalk at 8th St., 800/282-9709 for reservations only, www .lankfordhotel.com) is a sedate and slightly creaky three-story lodging right on the boardwalk. Built in 1924, it was one of the original boardwalk hotels and is still run by relatives of the builder, Mary Quillen. The hotel welcomes guests with reasonable rates—though if you're part of the party-all-night crowd, this may not be the place for you. The rooms have private baths and air-conditioning. An ocean view ($72–120) isn't much more than a side room ($66–114). Side suites of two rooms and a bath are ideal for families ($107–175).

The **Lankford Lodge,** just around the corner on 8th Street, 100 feet from the boardwalk, has rooms with private baths and air-conditioning. Rooms run $83–127, two-room suites (one bath) are $107–175. The Lankford Hotel and Lodge also offer apartments in nearby buildings.

The **Inn on the Ocean** (1001 Atlantic Ave., 410/289-8894 or 888/226-6223, www.innon theocean.com, year-round) is one of the prettiest renovated Victorian hotels on the beach. Attractively decorated rooms, all with private baths, air-conditioning, and breakfast, range $130–290, depending on the season (high season is roughly June–Sept.). Parking is available, along with bicycles, beach chairs, and umbrellas.

The **Spinnaker Motel** (18th St. at the boardwalk, 410/289-5444 or 800/638-3244, www .ocmotels.com, Mar.–Oct.) offers kitchenettes, cable TV, and two double beds in all units. Rates start out in May $45–115, go up in June to $155–185, peak in July–mid-August at $226, then slide down again to a low of $49–79 late September–October.

The ◖ **Lighthouse Club Hotel** (56th St. bayside, 410/524-5400 or 888/371-5400, www.fagers.com, year-round) is one of the most romantic places to stay in Ocean City. Built like an octagonal lighthouse (similar to the Thomas Point Lighthouse in the Chesapeake), the structure encloses 23 luxurious suites. Marble baths, hot tubs, Caribbean-style custom decor, wet bars, and refrigerators are in each suite (some have fireplaces); most have views of Isle of Wight Bay. Though "in town," the hotel is built on the wetlands of Fager's Island, and the feel is of being much more secluded than the location would suggest. Fager's Island restaurant is connected to the hotel by a footbridge, and guests receive passes for Ocean City Health & Racquet Club, a short drive away. When I stayed there, the weather seemed like a dark and sultry, but the building seemed like a safe haven in any storm, and the rooms are more like apartments. Ask about getaway specials throughout the year that include all meals. The lowest rates of the year are $99–139, in effect January 2–March 30. High-season rates (June 15–Oct. 4) range $224–305 per night. Breakfast is included, and the hotel offers specials throughout the year.

The Edge (60th St. on the bay, 410/524-5400, ext. 4021, or 888/371-5400, www.fagers.com, year-round) is the Fager empire's newest hotel, built for luxury. Twelve suites with panoramic water views, Jacuzzis, feather beds, and natural soaps and lotions are named according to decor: South Beach, Left Bank, The Jungle, and so on. Tariffs range $209–439 per night, depending on time of year.

Condos and Apartments

These are ideal for larger groups and longer stays. Some services, such as **Summer Beach Condos** (410/289-4669 or 800/678-5668, www.seagateoc.com), only handle rentals from a specific property (in this case, Seagate, a condo community three blocks from the beach). **Ocean City Weekly Rentals** (800/851-8909, www.ocwr.com) handles a number of properties for weekly, weekend, and midweek packages. **Holiday Real Estate** (800/638-2102, www.holidayoc.com) will send a rental catalog. They also handle multiple properties in the area.

The same people who manage the Lankford Hotel, mentioned above (800/282-9709, www .lanfordhotel.com), also rent out the **Sea Robin Apartments** on Eighth Street in a two-story older home 100 feet away from the boardwalk on Baltimore Street, the main route through town. The Sea Robin includes two apartments: one two-bedroom ($269–378 per day, $788–1,080 per week) and one three-bedroom ($411–504 per day, $1040–1,613 per week). Both apartments feature living and dining rooms, bath, and kitchen.

The Commander Hotel rents apartments within the hotel and in separate buildings, as do Phillips Beach Plaza, Dunes Manor, and Castle in the Sand. The **Sovereign Seas Condominiums** (two-bedroom/two-bath units half a block from the beach run $1,885 per week) are close to—and managed by—Castle in the Sand (410/289-6846 or 800/522-7263, www.castleinthesand.com). **Wagner Cottage** (one bedroom, one bath, $1,495 per week) is one of Castle in the Sand's cottage apartments and townhouses in the vicinity of 37th Street; all are rented by the week.

Camping

Ocean City Travel Park (105 70th St., 410/524-7601) is the only campground in Ocean City and is open year-round. It's one block from the beach and near the local bus service. It features all hookups, a laundry, and a camp store, and welcomes both RVs (no dump station) and tents.

Frontier Town (Rte. 611 and Stephen Decatur Hwy., 410/641-0880 or 800/228-5590), the Western theme park mentioned above, has all facilities for RVs and tents, and is open April–mid-October.

Additional camping is available at Assateague National Park and Assateague State Park.

FOOD
Cafés and Light Fare

Mad Hatter's Cafe (25th St. between Baltimore and Philadelphia Aves., 410/289-6267) serves deli fare (including vegetarian items) to eat in or take out—they also offer free delivery. Prices average $9.

Beach Food

For the best sand-and-sea cuisine, look to Ocean City's holy triumvirate: Dumser's, Thrasher's, and Fisher's.

Dumser's Drive-In (49th St. and Coastal Hwy., 410/524-1588) has been around since 1939. The restaurant is justifiably famous for its homemade ice cream, serving up big milkshakes, floats, sodas, sundaes, and cones. For lunch and dinner, there's a malt-shop menu with sandwiches and subs (average $8).

Thrasher's, with several locations on the boardwalk, is known for its french fries. Other beach eats, like corn dogs on a stick, are also available (under $5).

Fisher's, also on the boardwalk in several locations, is the place for caramel corn and sweets (under $5).

There's an outlet for everything these days. The **Jerky Outlet** (12842 U.S. 50, just over the bridge in West Ocean City, 410/213-1830) features Polish sausage, as well as a plethora of dried meats and a deli.

Buffets

The **Paul Revere Smorgasbord** (2nd St. and boardwalk, 410/524-1776) is a cherished hangout for the college crowd and families on a budget. The all-you-can-eat colonial feast Friday–Saturday is $9.99 for adults, less for kids, and even cheaper if you get there between 4 and 4:30 P.M. There's plenty of meat, plenty of fish, and lots of carbs—gourmet it's not, but you'll be fortified for several busy days.

Though it can't match the prices at Paul Revere's, **Embers Restaurant & Nite Club** (24th St. and Coastal Hwy., 410/289-3322) is a huge place with an all-you-can-eat seafood buffet with prime rib bar and breakfast buffet plus à la carte dishes ($12–30). It's open 2–11 P.M. March–October.

Jonah & the Whale Seafood Buffet (boardwalk and 26th St., 410/524-2722) is another big place with an all-you-can-eat seafood buffet, including a raw bar, dessert and salad bars, and a prime rib carving station. Prices are similar to Embers. It's open 4–9 P.M. mid-May–mid-September and offers early-bird specials.

Asian

Charlie Chiangs (5401 Coastal Hwy., 410/723-4600) advertises Hunan and Szechwan cuisine, but the menu concentrates on Mandarin-style favorites—General Tso's chicken, kung pao trio (chicken, beef, and shrimp), and O.C. specialties such as golden softshell crabs. It's open for lunch and dinner every day, and entrées average $14.

The Rice House (Rtes. 50 and 611, Teal Marsh Shopping Center, West Ocean City, 410/213-8388) serves a full Chinese menu ($9) in addition to sushi. It's open for lunch and dinner daily.

Asian Garden (1509 Philadelphia Ave., 410/289-7423) covers a lot of bases. Its menu features Chinese, Nepalese, and Indian dishes. It's open for dinner daily, and entrées average $11.

Italian

Tutti Gusti (3324 Coastal Hwy., 410/289-3318, www.ocean-city.com/tuttigusti, dinner Wed.–Mon.) gets my vote for the best food in town. Whole roasted garlic and olive oil accompanies fresh bread, and the housemade pappardelle pasta bathed in fresh Bolognese tomato sauce is excellent. It features a full range of Italian specialties and desserts. Entrées range $14–24. Tutti Gusti is open during the summer high season (until Oct. 15) and plans to stay open all year. Several patrons recommend the "weapons grade" martini. Reservations are a good idea.

O.C. Traditional

The restaurant most people associate with Ocean City is **Phillips Crab House** (21st and Coastal Hwy., 410/289-6821, lunch and dinner April–Oct.). Other locations are Phillips by the Sea (boardwalk and 13th St. in Phillips Beach Plaza Hotel, 410/289-9121, lunch and dinner Mar.–Dec.) and Phillips Seafood House (141st St. and Coastal Hwy., 410/250-1200, lunch and dinner Feb.–Nov.). You'll see the Phillips name a lot in Maryland. The restaurants employ so many people that the company imports help from overseas and provides inexpensive housing for them in Ocean City. The empire started with A. E. Phillips, a waterman from Fishing Creek on Hooper's Island. His grandson Brice moved to Ocean City in 1956 and opened a fresh crab takeout on 21st and Coastal Highway. It's still in operation, filling a corner of the larger restaurant, which is decorated in what the employees call "early Shirley," Shirley being Mrs. Phillips: carousel horses and Victorian stained-glass windows. Phillips serves a full menu (entrées average $18), but it's known for the buffet. It features snow crab, steamed blue crab, raw clams and oysters, cooked shrimp, and lots more, for around $30. You might want to wash it all down with an Eastern Shore Lemonade: citron vodka, triple sec, sour mix, and 7-Up.

You'll find many more locals than tourists at the **Hobbit** (101 81st St., 410/524-8100, dinner daily $26). It's the kind of dark wood/oak tables/big plates place that has kept people coming back for decades.

Crab Alley Restaurant and Seafood Market (9703 Golf Course Rd. and Sunset Ave., West Ocean City, 410/213-7800, lunch and dinner daily year-round, $12–30) is another eatery that's popular with locals. It's off the beaten path—on the west side, a few blocks south of Route 50. Though the restaurant serves a typical seafood menu, the ultra-fresh fare is brought in by local watermen.

Nouvelle Cuisine

◖ Galaxy 66 Bar & Grille (6601 Coastal Hwy., 410/723-6762, lunch and dinner daily year-round, $16–36) could be set in a major city; its sharply designed blue-and-gold, astronomically correct interior looks as if it's been plucked out of New York or San Francisco. The food tastes as good as it looks, and the wine list is sophisticated—in fact, it won a *Wine Spectator* Award of Excellence.

GETTING AROUND

The most common way to get to Ocean City is by car, though the area is serviced by a municipal airport three miles west (12724 Airport Rd., Berlin, 410/213-2471). Taxi service and car rentals are available at the airport.

Ocean City has wisely instituted a public transportation system that operates along the Coastal Highway January–late September, 24 hours a day. **The BUS** runs every 10 minutes 6 A.M.–noon and every 5–7 minutes noon–3 A.M., and every 20 minutes 3–6 A.M. May–September. You can catch it every other block from South First to 141st Streets on Philadelphia Avenue (which becomes the Coastal Highway as it proceeds north) and Baltimore Avenue. Two dollars (exact change) buys unlimited use within a 24-hour period. Call 410/723-1606 for more information. A handicapped bus is also available 7 A.M.–11 P.M., daily; call 410/723-1606 24 hours in advance of pickup time.

INFORMATION

Ocean City does a good job with promotion. For an information packet, contact the **Ocean City Department of Tourism** (4001 Coastal Hwy., Ocean City, MD 21842, 800/626-2326, www.ococean.com).

Assateague Island

Assateague is a 33-mile-long sandy barrier island, originally created by glacial movements at the end of the last ice age, and continually recreated by wave and wind action. Before 1933, Assateague was connected to Ocean City, part of the peninsula that extended from Fenwick Island in Delaware. During that year, a powerful storm removed a shallow sand spit, and might have replaced it if it weren't for human efforts to deepen and widen the subsequent channel.

It's doubtful that the island was a place of permanent habitation by the local Assateague Indians, though the first European to report on it in 1524, Giovanni da Verrazano, found it "very beautiful." He promptly kidnapped an Indian boy who was attempting to hide, but gave up on a young girl of 18 "because of the loud shrieks she uttered as we attempted to lead her away." Welcome to the New World.

Over the years, small settlements grew on the island, but most faded away before 1900. As early as 1935, the federal government surveyed the island as a possible park, but no action was taken. Developers began building dwellings on the island in the 1950s, leveling the dunes for road access. Thanks to the lack of impediments, another storm literally floated the houses away in 1962.

At that point, the government did step in. Today, the island consists of three major public areas: Assateague Island National Seashore, managed by the National Park Service (the entire island, open year-round); Assateague State Park, managed by the Maryland Department of Natural Resources (the northern end); and Chincoteague National Wildlife Refuge, managed by the U.S. Fish and Wildlife Service (the southern end). There is no access from the northern end of the island to the southern end: the Maryland side is accessed via Route 611 on the mainland, the Virginia side by Route 175. The 680-acre State Park offers swimming, surf fishing, surf boarding, bathhouses with hot showers, a bait and tackle shop, camping, and a snack bar. Because of the wildlife population, pets are not permitted on most of the island.

Chincoteague Island does not allow camping in the wildlife refuge, though it's an excellent birding and wildlife spotting area. Some hunting is allowed on the Virginia side during September. The refuge was purchased with duck stamp revenues in 1943 to provide a protected environment for migrating waterfowl. The **Chincoteague Refuge Visitor Center** off Maddox Boulevard (follow signs from Route 175) offers guided walks and programs; a tour bus is available. Contact the refuge manager (Chincoteague National Wildlife Refuge, P.O. Box 62, Chincoteague, VA 23336, 757/336-6122) for more information.

Many visitors come to see the island's large herds of wild horses. The origin of the sturdy little animals has been disputed, though it's agreed that they roamed the island as early as the 17th century. Some say a Spanish or English ship floundered off the southern end of the island and the animals swam ashore; others claim that the horses are descended from domesticated stock that was grazed on the island (a handy way for local planters to avoid mainland taxes and fencing requirements). Today, a fence separates the herds across the state line. The Maryland herd is protected by the state and roams freely throughout the park, though they stay well away from groups of people on foot. The Chincoteague Volunteer Fire Company owns the Virginia herd; each year, horses are rounded up and many of the foals are sold at the Pony Penning and auction, held on the last Wednesday–Thursday In July. The funds support the fire company, and the animals are prized for their strength and longevity.

RECREATION
Water Sports
Assateague State Park provides lifeguards throughout the summer on its **swimming** beaches. Both visitors centers present **surf fishing** demonstrations during the summer; no saltwater license is required. Fishing is prohibited on lifeguarded beaches, and an after-hours fishing permit is required on the Virginia end of the island. **Crabbing, clamming, and shell collecting** are popular pastimes; clamming is especially good on Maryland's bay side. **Canoes** may be rented from a concession at the end of Bayside Drive on the Maryland side. The bay is quite shallow, and canoeists and boaters may not land anywhere on the island's Virginia end other than Fishing Point September 1–March 14.

Hiking and Biking
On the Maryland side, hikers may use several short self-guided nature trails, or trek on the beach to Ocean City or south on the off-road vehicle (ORV) trail to the Virginia border. Cyclists can enjoy three miles of paved bike paths along Bayberry Drive; bike rentals are available from a concession at the end of Bayside Drive. In Virginia, 15 miles of trails wind through marshes and forests, and include a path to the

Assateague Lighthouse. Hikers may also enjoy miles of undisturbed beach north of the Toms Cove Visitor Center. Half the trails are paved for cyclists, and a bike path leads from the town of Chincoteague to the refuge. In fact, bicycling is encouraged in the refuge during the busy summer weekends.

Off-Road Vehicles

ORV zones are posted and maps are available at the visitors centers and refuge headquarters. The National Seashore (410/641-3030) requires permits and strict specifications for ORVs. You can also contact the Assateague Island National Seashore (7206 National Seashore Ln., Berlin, MD 21811) for information.

Camping

The Maryland side features the **Barrier Island Visitor Center,** maintained by the Assateague Island National Seashore. A live touch tank, exhibits, guided walks, and other programs are available to visitors. This is also the place to inquire about backcountry camping: two oceanside sites and four bayside camps are backpack- and canoe-accessible. They have chemical toilets but no drinking water, and are free with a parking and backcountry use permit. The nearest is four miles from parking. For more information, stop by the visitors center or contact Assateague Island National Sea-shore (7206 National Seashore Ln., Berlin, MD 21811, 410/641-1441, www.nps.gov/asis).

In addition, the State Park offers two car campgrounds, Oceanside and Bayside, which are equipped with chemical toilets, drinking water, and cold showers. There is a dump station but no hookups, and a few sites are for tents only. Some are open year-round. Reservations are necessary; Reserve America (877/444-6777, www.recreation.gov) takes reservations up to six months in advance of the date you want to camp April 15–October 15. The State Park campground can accommodate any size camping unit, but may be closed during the winter. Reservations for a full week may be made only during the summer. For more information and reservations, contact Assateague State Park (7307 Stephen Decatur Hwy., Berlin, MD 21811, 410/641-2120).

Chincoteague Island does not allow camping in the wildlife refuge.

INFORMATION

Worchester County covers a lot of ground, from scenic Snow Hill to the sandy reaches of Assateague and Ocean City. For comprehensive information, contact **Worchester County Tourism** (104 West Market St., Snow Hill, MD 21863, 410/632-3110 or 800/852-0335, www .visitworchester.org). Ocean City's tourist site is also a good source for most of the county.

MOON MARYLAND'S EASTERN SHORE
Avalon Travel
a member of the Perseus Books Group
1700 Fourth Street
Berkeley, CA 94710, USA
www.moon.com

Editor: Shaharazade Husain
Series Manager: Kathryn Ettinger
Copy Editor: Mia Lipman
Graphics Coordinator: Stefano Boni
Production Coordinator: Darren Alessi
Cover Designer: Stefano Boni
Map Editor: Kevin Anglin
Cartographers: Kat Bennett, Chris Markiewicz

ISBN-13: 978-1-59880-409-6

Text © 2008 by Joanne Miller.
Maps © 2008 by Avalon Travel
All rights reserved.

ABOUT THE AUTHOR

Joanne Miller

Joanne Miller lives and writes her own adventures in full color, whether watching the fiery sun set under full sail near St. Michaels, dodging feisty crabs on Smith Island's oyster-shell roads, or feeling the burn while climbing Baltimore's Washington Monument. Her interests in fine food and wine, art, environmental issues, and American history come through in her writing – every place has its story, and Joanne makes the landscape come alive through words and pictures.

Joanne first glimpsed the elite Maryland suburbs north of Washington D.C. on the last leg of a coast-to-coast trip after securing a BA in anthropology in California. In the following years, she visited the Tidewater to crack crab in Ocean City and indulge in fantasies of life among the super-rich in Winterthur. Joanne keeps hope alive for the day when crabcakes are considered a diet food.

Joanne is the author of *Moon Pennsylvania, Moon Maryland & Delaware,* and *Moon Chesapeake Bay,* and is a frequent contributor to *Writer's Market* and *Novel & Short Story Writer's Market.* Currently, she is working on a novel of old San Francisco, *The Richest Gal in Boom Town.*